Juvenile Instructor Office

Early Scenes in Church History

Eighth Book of the Faith Promoting Series

Juvenile Instructor Office

Early Scenes in Church History
Eighth Book of the Faith Promoting Series

ISBN/EAN: 9783337260019

Printed in Europe, USA, Canada, Australia, Japan

Cover: Foto ©Lupo / pixelio.de

More available books at **www.hansebooks.com**

EARLY SCENES

IN

CHURCH HISTORY.

EIGHTH BOOK OF THE

FAITH-PROMOTING SERIES.

Designed for the Instruction and Encouragement of
of Young Latter-day Saints.

———◆◆◆———

JUVENILE INSTRUCTOR OFFICE,
Salt Lake City,
1882.

Copyright applied for at the Office of the Librarian of Congress, at Washington, D. C., by G. C. Lambert.

PREFACE.

MANY deaths have occurred within the last few years among the veteran members of our Church. Numbers of persons have recently passed away who were connected with the Church during the early years of its existence, and whose lives were filled with scenes and incidents of the most interesting nature. Their wonderful experience so far as known is appreciated by their intimate friends, in whose memories it is embalmed, but it will hereafter only be known as tradition, for, as a rule, they have left no written testimony or record of their lives to show to future generations what they have seen or passed through. We have scarcely ever heard of the death of such a person without a feeling of regret that the important scenes of which he was a witness while living were not better known, and that a definite and accurate account of them had not been written before his death.

A short time since we conceived the idea of publishing a volume of the "Faith-Promoting Series," entitled EARLY SCENES IN CHURCH HISTORY, to be made up of such incidents of appropriate nature as we could obtain from early members of the Church.

Of course we were aware that a single volume of the size contemplated could not describe a tithe of the interesting scenes of a faith-promoting nature with which the early history of the Church abounded, but not until we had started the compilation did we realize to the full extent the vastness of the field which we had entered upon. We gathered the incidents contained in the present volume at random (mostly from verbal narratives), compiled them very hastily, with too little regard perhaps for variety, and feel that we have hardly made a commencement at recounting the early scenes of which a record should be perpetuated.

In compiling this volume no effort has been made at selecting scenes of a marvelous or sensational character; the aim has rather been to mention such incidents as would tend to show how the power of God was manifested in behalf of the Saints in those early days, and thereby promote faith among the young, for whose benefit this Series is published. Nor is it to be supposed that such scenes as are herein described have been confined to any particular period of our Church's history. As wonderful incidents of special providence could be related of the present age as of that which is past. The power of God is as manifest now in shaping the destiny of His Saints, in preserving their lives and in answering their prayers as it ever has been. The faithful never had greater cause to rejoice nor the wicked to tremble than they have at the present time. That the perusal of this volume may cause those into whose hands it may come to be more faithful and devoted to the cause of God, is the earnest desire of

THE PUBLISHER.

CONTENTS.

"SHOW US A SIGN."

My Sister's Hip Broken—No Hopes of Ever Being Able to Walk—Our Family Embrace the Gospel—Scoffers Demand as a Sign that my Sister be Healed—Elder Brackinbury's Death—Warned by the Spirit of the Body-Snatchers' Designs—Caught in the Act of Robbing the Grave—My Brother's Death—My Sister Healed—The Healing Fails to Convince the Unbelievers. Page 9.

CONTEST WITH EVIL SPIRITS.

The Savior's Promise—Sent on a Mission When a Boy—Conference in Burke's Garden—A Girl Apparently Stricken With Death—My Fright at Being Asked to Administer to Her—Prompted by the Spirit to Cast the Devil Out of Her—The Evil Spirit Leaves Her and Enters Two Others—Six Elders Contend With the Evil Spirit for Thirty-Six Hours—Its Final Banishment. Page 12.

EARLY EXPERIENCE OF A. O. SMOOT.

CHAPTER I.

Sickly Condition when Young—Healed According to Elder Patten's Prediction—Labor as a Missionary with Elder Woodruff—Severe Sickness—Healed Under the Administration of my Brethren—A Mission to the Southern States—Removal to Far West—Mission to Missouri and Arkansas—Opposed by a Baptist Deacon—Terrible Judgment upon Himself and Family—John Houston, the Infidel—Far West Besieged—Taken Prisoner. Page 17.

CHAPTER II.

Married while a Prisoner of War—Property Confiscated—Removal to Quincy—First Hard Work—Removal to Montrose—Mission to Tennessee—Shot at—Camp, my Champion—A Lawyer and his Mob—Appeal to Masons for Help—Ready Response—Camp's Vengeance on the Lawyer—News of Martyrdom—Return to Nauvoo—Brigham Young Inspired—Another Mission South—Blessings in the Temple—Journey to Salt Lake Valley.   Page 21.

CHAPTER III.

Almost Lost in the Atlantic—Narrowly Escape the *Saluda* Disaster—Nearly Dead with the Cholera—Healed in Answer to Prayer—Blown up with a Keg of Powder—A Sick Woman Healed—Elder Patten's Remarkable Prediction Fulfilled—A Man Almost Dead Recovers on Being Baptized.   Page 26.

SCENES IN THE BRITISH MISSION.

CHAPTER I.

Elder Halliday Applied to for Help by a Sister whose Son is Dying—Not Able to go, he Gives the Lady his Handkerchief and Promises her the Child Shall Live—The Child Revives from Apparent Death by the Woman's Faith and Prayer—Preaching in Penzance—Discouragement and Want—Strange Conduct of a Lady Attending the Meeting—Invitation to go to St. Just—Gift of Tongues and Interpretation Given to Elder Halliday, Through which he Receives a Revelation—Revelation Literally Fulfilled.
Page 31.

CHAPTER II.

Elder Elias Morris Falls with a Scaffold a Distance of Thirty Feet Without Being Hurt—Gift of Healing Possessed by Elder Abel Evans—A Woman Healed who had Her Face Eaten Away by a Cancer—Storm at Sea Rebuked—A Broken Leg Cured—A Broken Skull Mended—Fever on Shipboard Stopped by the Prayer of Faith.   Page 36.

CHAPTER III.

Elder John Parry's Statement—His Brother's Testimony and Death—His Sister's Reproof and Death—Embrace the Gospel—His Sleep Troubled—A Remedy and Lesson—Orson Spencer Healed—Providential Help—Escape from a Mob—Cancer in a Man's Face Cured by Laying on of Hands— Preserved from Mobs.   Page 42.

CHAPTER IV.

John T. Evans' Statement—A Sick and Helpless Woman Healed on Being Baptized—Relapse and Death after Apostasy—Saints Required to Renounce their Religion or Lose their Situations—Cholera Epidemic—Healed According to Faith—Private Discussion with a Malignant Preacher, who Takes the Cholera and Begs the Elders to Cure Him—Healed and then Baptized—Curious Manner in which Food and Lodging were Provided.   Page 49.

CHAPTER V.

Judgment Upon Opposers—Two Men Killed by their Horses—Horrible Death of Another—Eight Preachers go Down After Opposing Elder Evans—A Man Saved from Bleeding to Death by the Prayer of Faith—A Sister Healed—Woman Cured of a Bloody Issue on Being Baptized—Escape the Fury of a Mob by the Spirit's Warning—A Warning Through the Gift of Tongues.   Page 57.

CHAPTER VI.

Thomas D. Giles' Experience—His Head Crushed and Split Open by a Ton of Coal Falling Upon It—Healed by the Power of God—A Deaf and Dumb Man Receives His Hearing and Speech on Being Baptized, etc.   Page 62.

CHAPTER VII.

Scene in the Experience of Wm. J. Smith—A Strange Prophecy and Its Wonderful Fulfillment.   Page 68.

REMARKABLE HEALINGS.

Martin H. Peck's Testimony of a Number of Remarkable Cases of Healing—A Broken Arm, a Crushed Leg, etc., Healed Immediately. Page 70.

PHILO DIBBLE'S NARRATIVE.

CHAPTR I.

His Early Life—Conversion—Curious Signs—Joseph Removes to Kirtland—Wonderful Manifestations—A Miraculous Case of Healing—Sidney Rigdon in Darkness—Joseph Predicts that the Evil One will Handle Him, and the Prediction is Fulfilled. Page 74.

CHAPTER II.

Removal to Missouri—The Saints' Guns Purchased for Mobocrats by a Sectarian Preacher—Attack of the Mob on the Whitmer Settlement—The Writer Shot—Subsequent Exposure and Suffering—Critical Condition—Healed Miraculously—How Zion's Camp was preserved on Fishing River—A Vision. Page 81.

CHAPTER III.

Militia Organized at Far West—Liberty Pole Struck by Lightning—General Atchison Defends the Prophet in a Lawsuit—Atchison Removed from Office for being Friendly to the Saints—Far West Besieged—Leaders of the Saints Betrayed for a Price—Escape to Quincy. Page 87.

CHAPTER IV.

Rent a Farm—Sickness—Providential Recovery—Inspired to Preach—Removal to Nauvoo—Death of my Wife—Second Marriage—Premonition of Death—Warning from the Prophet—A Dream and its Fulfillment—A Prophecy and its Fulfillment—Evil Spirits Cast out of a Man—Joseph Smith's Trust in the Lord. Page 91.

"SHOW US A SIGN."

BY B. F. JOHNSON

MY SISTER'S HIP BROKEN—NO HOPES OF EVER BEING ABLE TO WALK—OUR FAMILY EMBRACE THE GOSPEL—SCOFFERS DEMAND AS A SIGN THAT MY SISTER BE HEALED—ELDER BRACKINBURY'S DEATH—WARNED BY THE SPIRIT OF THE BODY-SNATCHERS' DESIGNS—CAUGHT IN THE ACT OF ROBBING THE GRAVE—MY BROTHER'S DEATH—MY SISTER HEALED—THE HEALING FAILS TO CONVINCE THE UNBELIEVERS.

ABOUT the year 1830, when I was twelve years of age, Nancy, my eldest sister, was thrown from a horse, and had her hip broken.

The bone was broken so near the socket that it could not be set, and physicians all agreed that it would be impossible for her ever again to walk upon that leg, or in any degree to recover its use, as ossification had taken place without a connection of the bones and they had slipped past each other, making the broken limb nearly an inch shorter than the other. She walked upon two crutches, and for years was not able to bring upon the broken limb weight sufficient to hurt the finger of a small child, if placed under her foot.

In the year 1831, my brothers Joel H. and David received the gospel in Amherst, Ohio, and in the fall of the same year my brother David brought to us the Book of Mormon, near Fredonia, State of New York.

Soon afterwards my brother Joel, with A. W. Babbitt—then only a boy, came also, and was followed by Elders Brack inbury and Durfee. Elder Brackinbury was an earnest and powerful preacher, and all the Elders seemed filled with the spirit of the Lord. Many received their testimony, and my mother and Lyman R. Shearman, a brother-in-law, were the first to be baptized.

Priest and people came out to oppose the work, and would scoffingly ask, "Why, if miracles can be performed, do you not heal Sister Nancy?" Many would also say: "If they would only heal Sister Nancy we would all believe!"

My sister was a young woman of excellent mind and character. Having a good common education, she had for some years taught our district summer school, and, being religiously inclined, had joined the Freewill Baptist church. Like my mother, who was also a religious woman, she was not only respected, but was beloved by all who knew her. But, although she had obeyed the gospel, the time had not come for her release from her crutches by the healing power of God. The wicked were seeking it for a sign, as in the days of our Savior, when they followed Him even to His crucifixion, demanding that He come down from the cross, as a sign, to prove to them that He was the Son of God; yet no sign was given except that of their overthrow and destruction.

After a few weeks of successful preaching and baptizing, Elder Brackinbury was taken violently sick, and, within a few days, died of the bilious cholic.

To us, then young and inexperienced members of the Church, his death came as a trial to our faith, as well as a very great grief. To think that so good a man, in such a field of useful labor, and far away from his home and family, should be permitted to die, and that too so suddenly, was naturally a test to the faith and integrity of so young a branch.

Although the grave had closed over his body and we were in deep sorrow, our enemies were not satisfied, for while we were assembled in the evening after his burial, to talk and pray and mourn together, the spirit of revelation said to my brother David that they were then digging up the body of Brother Brackinbury for dissection.

My brothers with others quickly started, and proceeding rapidly to the grave about one mile away, found three men there who had unearthed the coffin and were just dragging the corpse from under its lid. As our party approached they sprang out of the grave and fled.

David, then a stripling of about twenty years, pursued them, and like a young lion, grappled with, captured and brought back as a prisoner one of the most powerful young men of the country—not only much older but nearly double his size—a student of medicine in our native town.

The prisoner was afterwards committed by a magistrate, and put under bonds to appear at his trial.

These, with other unhappy events, caused us to desire to leave our native place and gather with the Saints at Kirtland, which we did in the spring of 1833. In the summer of that same year it was proposed to build the Kirtland Temple, and as it was designed at first to build it of brick, my three eldest brothers, with those of us who were younger, engaged in making the brick for that purpose; and there brother David, who was then about twenty-two years of age, became a martyr to the great and good cause. Through his ambition to perform more labor than he was able to endure, and by over-exertion in procuring the wood, he bled at the lungs and died the same fall. He bore a faithful testimony of the gospel being again revealed, and spoke with the gift of tongues with his latest breath, which was interpreted by Don Carlos Smith, the Prophet's brother, who was present at the time.

About this time the Spirit of the Lord seemed to be poured out upon the Saints in Kirtland. There families often met together to "speak of the Lord," and the gifts of the gospel were enjoyed in rich abundance. As yet my sister Nancy had never, since her hip had been broken, taken one step unaided by her crutches; but the time had now come for her release.

She was commanded by Elder Jared Carter—then a man of mighty faith—to arise, leave her crutches and walk.

She arose in faith, full of joy, and was from that hour made whole, and never again did she walk upon crutches or lean upon a staff.

The same fall I returned on a visit to my native town, full of a desire that our old neighbors, as well as my young associates, should embrace the truth; for I felt sure that they would believe my testimony that my sister was healed, and, as they had promised, accept the gospel.

I was full of hope, although I was but a boy, that they would all be converted through my testimony; but alas! there were none to be converted—no one to accept the great truths of the gospel. They believed my statement that my sister had become well and was walking unaided upon her broken limb, yet, to their understanding, "some natural cause had produced the effect," and they were unbelievers still.

When again, as a missionary, I returned to the place of my birth and preached to those same persons the gospel, bearing a faithful testimony, they were glad to see me, and treated me with great kindness, yet no one was converted to the truth, for signs had failed to make them believe.

CONTEST WITH EVIL SPIRITS.

BY H. G. B.

THE SAVIOR'S PROMISE—SENT ON A MISSION WHEN A BOY—CONFERENCE IN BURKE'S GARDEN—A GIRL APPARENTLY STRICKEN WITH DEATH—MY FRIGHT AT BEING ASKED TO ADMINISTER TO HER—PROMPTED BY THE SPIRIT TO CAST THE DEVIL OUT OF HER—THE EVIL SPIRIT LEAVES HER AND ENTERS TWO OTHERS—SIX ELDERS CONTEND WITH THE EVIL SPIRIT FOR THIRTY-SIX HOURS—ITS FINAL BANISHMENT.

JUST a few minutes before our Savior took His leave of the twelve apostles and ascended on high, He promised that certain gifts and blessings should be enjoyed by the believer. You will find this promise recorded in the 16th chapter of

A GIRL APPARENTLY STRICKEN WITH DEATH.

the gospel according to St. Mark, 17th and 18th verses. It is of one of these gifts that I wish to speak.

When on my first mission (in the year 1844), in the State of Virginia, we were attending a conference in Burke's Garden, Tazewell County. There were some ten or twelve Elders in attendance, most of whom had just arrived a week or two previous from Nauvoo, where they had, during the April Conference, been called and set apart for missions in Virginia. It was Sunday evening, some time early in May. Our conference had just closed, the last services of which were the ordinances of baptism and confirmation administered to several persons.

The Saints and strangers had dispersed to their homes, except some of the Saints who lived at a distance. A few of these had put up with Colonel Peter Litz, who, with his family, were members of the Church, and where also several of the Elders, myself included, were going to stay over night.

The time in the evening was what would be called early twilight. Some of the Elders had taken an evening stroll. At any rate, I was the only Elder that was about the house, when Sister Litz came to me (I was seated at the time out in the yard) very much excited, and said that one of the sisters who had come to stay over night, was taken suddenly and very severely sick, and she (Sister Litz) desired me to administer to her.

I was only a boy, yet in my teens, and with little or no experience, and had never been called upon, up to that time, to administer to the sick. I naturally shrank from the task, and would have given anything to have had some one to take it off my shoulders.

However, there was no escape for me—no other Elders were present, and she insisted that I should attend to the ordinance.

I followed Sister Litz into the house, and there lay the girl, stretched upon a bed, apparently lifeless, without breath or motion.

I asked Sister Litz what was the matter with the girl, but she could not tell.

"What can I do?" I thought. What could any one do? Nevertheless, I placed my hands upon her head, knowing full well if the Lord did not help me, that I would utterly fail in being able to say the first appropriate word, or exercise the least power.

As soon as I opened my mouth, I began to cast a devil out of her, which was farthest from my thoughts before I commenced. I commanded it, in the name of Jesus Christ, to come out of her, and not to return again. The evil spirit immediately departed from her, she being restored to her normal condition, seemingly as well as ever.

Not ten minutes after, the same evil spirit entered another girl. But during this interval Elder Robert Hamilton had returned from a walk, and was present at the time of the second attack, and was mouth with myself in casting it out.

In about the same time it would take a person to walk from one room to another, a third young sister was attacked, and in the same way exactly that the two first had been taken; and our administration had the same effect in relieving her as in the first two cases.

This third one was no sooner rid of the evil spirit, than it returned and took possession the second time of the one last before relieved of its power; and when it was cast out from this one, it took possession of the third one again, and so on, alternately, as well as I can remember, for three or four times. But the spirit never returned the second time to the first sister that was attacked that evening.

However, at the end of three or four hours, we separated the two girls, by taking one of them up stairs and into a room at the west end of the house, leaving the other in a room on the first floor at the east end, making the distance between as far as we could for both to occupy the same house, which was a large one.

In the meantime, one of the Elders from the house of one of the nearest neighbors had come in, so there were six of us in attendance, the names of whom were as follows: Robert Hamilton, James Park, Richard Kinnamon, Chapman Duncan, Alfred B. Lambson and myself.

A. B. Lambson, James Park and Richard Kinnamon, with

the father of the two girls (for they were sisters), watched with the one in the room on the first floor, while Robert Hamilton, Chapman Duncan and myself, with the mother, watched with the other in the upper room.

While possessed with this evil spirit, the girls would sometimes lay in a trance, motionless, and apparently without breathing, till we were ready to conclude they were dead, then they would come to and speak and sing in tongues, and talk about Priesthood and the endowments. At other times, they would choke up, ceasing to breathe until they were black in the face, and we thought they would surely die. Sometimes they would froth at the mouth and act like they were in a fit. If standing upon their feet when taken, they would fall to the floor and act like they were struggling for life with some unseen power. Altogether, these cases reminded us of the one recorded in Mark, 8th chapter, 14th to 29th verse, and other cases recorded in the New Testament.

We never made a failure when attempting to cast out this evil spirit from either of the girls. But invariably as soon as one of them was dispossessed, in the length of time it would take a person to walk from one room to the other, the spirit would take possession of the other, but never both at the same time, and both were operated upon alike, so we knew there was but one evil spirit to deal with; yet it seemed impossible to get rid of it, for the girls were possessed with it alternately for some thirty-six hours.

However, we took advantage of the Savior's explanation in the 9th chapter of Mark, before referred to, and fasted and prayed. After which, while the three of us up stairs were administering (Robert Hamilton being mouth) and commanding the devil (for such we were from the first convinced it was) to come out of her and return to its own place, Elder Duncan immediately interrupted, and said to Elder Hamilton, "Name the place; name the place!" (See Matthew, 8th chapter and 31st verse.)

This somewhat confused Elder Hamilton, who hesitated, when Elder Duncan called the name of a family who were near neighbors, and of whom not one us had thought in connection with these cases. Elder Hamilton repeated this name, and immediately the evil spirit departed, not only from the girl it then had possession of, but from the house. And in a moment all in the house felt and knew that they were rid of its power and influence and that it would not again return.

We all, by this time, knew something of the power of the adversary, for we had had an actual experience, indeed, a contest, that had left us weak and nearly worn out, to an extent that an actual corporal struggle with flesh and blood would not have so reduced us.

Why was the key to its departure given to Elder Duncan and not to Elder Hamilton, who was acting as mouthpiece at the time? is a question my young readers are ready to ask, as we asked one another at the time, and were not able to answer, and which I am unable to answer to this day.

And why was it necessary to give this demon the privilege to return to torment some other family?

This also I am unable to answer to my own satisfaction; but this much I can say: the family referred to was bitterly opposed to the gospel and its blessings, and to all those who taught, practiced, or enjoyed the same. A daughter of this family had been afflicted in a very singular way from her childhood. This girl had, in company with her parents and all the family (as they never left her alone), attended our baptismal meeting on Sunday evening, and her family spoke of her being and acting like a new person for two days after attending that meeting, often speaking of the good effect the witnessing of the ordinance of baptism had had upon her.

To all I have said in the foregoing, I was an eye and ear witness. All those who are living, who were present at the time this occurred, will remember the truth of what I have inscribed, though at the time we kept it from the world. I have written this experience for the benefit of the young Elders who are now abroad on missions, and for the benefit of the boys who may hereafter be called on to take missions, and any others who may glean any good from its perusal; and also as an evidence of the truth of the promise of Jesus to believers.

EARLY EXPERIENCE OF A. O. SMOOT.

CHAPTER I.

SICKLY CONDITION WHEN YOUNG—HEALED ACCORDING TO ELDER PATTEN'S PREDICTION—LABOR AS A MISSIONARY WITH ELDER WOODRUFF—SEVERE SICKNESS—HEALED UNDER THE ADMINISTRATION OF MY BRETHREN—A MISSION TO THE SOUTHERN STATES—REMOVAL TO FAR WEST—MISSION TO MISSOURI AND ARKANSAS—OPPOSED BY A BAPTIST DEACON—TERRIBLE JUDGMENT UPON HIMSELF AND FAMILY—JOHN HOUSTON, THE INFIDEL—FAR WEST BESIEGED—TAKEN PRISONER.

MY life has been an exceedingly active, busy one, but when my experience is compared with that of many of my brethren there is perhaps nothing very extraordinary about it. I have seen the power of God manifested in various ways, and have had all the testimonies that I could ask for of the divine character of the work instituted through Joseph Smith, with which I have been connected for almost half a century. But I have never seen anything that I could call very miraculous, nor have I sought for anything of the kind as an evidence of the truth of God's work. To me everything has seemed to come along naturally. And yet when all things are considered, my whole life might be regarded as miraculous. When I reflect upon the precarious condition of my health when a boy, and the indulgence with which I was then treated, and then upon what I have been enabled to endure and accomplish, through the blessings of God since, there is something rather remarkable about it to me.

I was born on the 17th of February, 1815, in Owenton, Owen Co., Kentucky. Both the town and County in which

I was born were named after my great-uncle, Abraham Owen, in whose honor I was named. He was killed in the battle of Tippecanoe, while serving under General Harrison, who was afterwards President of the United States. Abraham Owen's sister, my great-aunt, was Stonewall Jackson's mother, so that General Jackson and I were second-cousins.

From my early childhood, almost from my infancy, I was afflicted with a lung disease, and supposed to be in consumption. Indeed, I was so bad a great deal of the time that my life was despaired of. When I was about nine years old my death seemed so imminent that my burial clothes were made. However, I rallied somewhat, but not to be able to do any work. I had a great desire to live, and also to know if the Lord had a church upon the earth, and I investigated the various doctrines professed by those with whom I came in contact, but could never feel satisfied to join any of the religious sects.

When I attained my twentieth year, and while I was still very sickly, Elders David W. Patten and Warren Parrish visited the part where I resided, as missionaries, and I became convinced of the correctness of the doctrines which they taught and embraced the same, being baptized by Elder Parrish and confirmed by Elder Patten. Brother Patten, in confirming me, promised that I should be healed of my infirmity and become a strong and powerful man. This prediction was verified to the letter; I began to grow strong immediately.

The following spring I was ordained a deacon and placed to preside over a small branch of the Church raised up by Elders Patten and Parrish, and on the 7th of the next April I was ordained an Elder under the hands of Brother Woodruff and started out with him preaching. I traveled with him in Kentucky and Tennessee until the early part of the following winter, when we left the South and went to Kirtland, Ohio, where I attended school with him and studied Greek and Latin.

The change of climate and a little carelessness on my part brought on an attack of typhoid fever and pleurisy, from which I suffered severely, and it was thought that I could not recover. Brother Woodruff, however, who was waiting upon me, called in Elders Brigham Young, Heber C. Kimball, Willard Richards, and Hyrum Smith, and the five laid their hands upon me and rebuked the disease and blessed me. While their hands were upon my head I fell into an easy sleep, and when I awoke my disease was entirely gone.

A few days after, I was advised by the Prophet Joseph to return to the Southern States and raise up a company of Saints and emigrate to Far West, Missouri. I accordingly went South, and in the month of May had succeeded in organizing a company of two hundred souls with about forty teams and started on our journey. The trip occupied about two months. We immediately set about making homes and soon began to get comfortable surroundings.

In January, 1838, I was called to fill a mission to the southern part of Missouri and throughout Arkansas. During this mission an incident occurred which I think worth relating. I was preaching one afternoon in the court-house at Yellsville, where I had also held meeting in the forenoon, when in the midst of my discourse I was interrupted by a Baptist deacon, who arose and exclaimed: "That young man is not quoting the scripture correctly."

I was speaking at the time upon the authenticity of the Book of Mormon. I was also enjoying an unusual flow of the Holy Spirit, and felt more calm and collected at this interruption than I otherwise would have done. I deliberately opened the Bible and read therefrom the very passages which I had previously quoted verbatim, and cited the chapter and verse.

At this the Baptist took his seat, but I had not proceeded much farther with my remarks when I again had occasion to quote from the scriptures, and lest I again should be found fault with, I opened the Bible and read from it, when the deacon, a second time arose and declared that it was not from King James' translation of the Bible that I was quoting, but "Joe Smith's golden Bible," etc.

Several of the audience immediately ordered him to be still and let the young man proceed, as they wanted to hear the preaching.

Again he became quiet, but soon broke forth in a perfect rage, said I was lying, and denounced, in a rather incoherent manner,

"Joe Smith" and his "golden bible," and the "Mormons" as "chicken thieves"and "hog stealers," etc.

A number of persons immediately surrounded him as if they intended to thrust him out, and lest they should use violence I began to plead for him, and requested them to allow him to retire quietly. I added, however, that I was there on my Father's business, commissioned to proclaim the gospel, and if he did not speedily repent the Lord would rebuke him and the judgment of God would overtake him. At this he turned and rushed from the room almost foaming with rage.

He had four drunken sons in the town and he proceeded to hunt them up to incite them to mob me. Just then a fire broke out in the Baptist meeting house, and on hearing the alarm I adjourned the meeting for one hour.

In the audience was a Major John Houston, a brother of the celebrated Sam Houston, who was in command of a military post near by. He had boarded a few days at the same place that I had, and had therefore become somewhat acquainted with me.

He followed the deacon and advised him against molesting me, telling him if he persisted in it he would have to take him in charge. The deacon concluded to desist but raged, and cursed "Joe Smith" and the "golden bible"and the young preacher, and everything connected with him as he proceeded home, and on entering his house, almost immediately fell dead and turned black.

In this condition he lay for two days, no one, not even his own sons, daring to go near him until, a Campbellite preacher, who also had happened to be one of my audience, and who had heard of his condition, came to me and informed me of it. I went with him to Major Houston, and through his influence some persons were employed to go and bury the dead man.

Within a week from the time of the deacon's death his wife also died, and his sons kept up their drunken spree until they had run through four thousand dollars of the money which their father had left and also other property.

Many of the people of the town regarded this series of calamities as the judgment of God, and even the Campbellite preacher admitted to me that it had very much the appearance of it.

Soon after these events transpired I returned to a place about twenty miles distant, to fill a previous appointment, and while there Major Houston was taken sick with the cholera. He felt that he was going to die, and wanted to have me sent for. I had conversed with him many times upon the subject of religion, and, though he professed to be an infidel, I could see that he was pricked in his heart but was too proud to acknowledge it. Shortly before he died he made a request that I should preach his funeral sermon, and on my return to Yellsville I did so, and I think I never had more of the Spirit of God in preaching in my life than I did on that occasion, infidel though he pretended to be.

I returned from this mission in the summer of 1838, and soon afterwards the troubles of the Saints with the Missouri mobocrats recommenced, in which I became earnestly engaged. After Far West had been besieged by the mob militia under General Clark and we had been compelled to surrender our arms, I was taken prisoner in company with many of my brethren.

CHAPTER II.

MARRIED WHILE A PRISONER OF WAR—PROPERTY CONFISCATED—REMOVAL TO QUINCY—FIRST HARD WORK—REMOVAL TO MONTROSE—MISSION TO TENNESSEE—SHOT AT—CAMP, MY CHAMPION—A LAWYER AND HIS MOB—APPEAL TO MASONS FOR HELP—READY RESPONSE—CAMP'S VENGEANCE ON THE LAWYER—NEWS OF MARTYRDOM—RETURN TO NAUVOO—BRIGHAM YOUNG INSPIRED—ANOTHER MISSION SOUTH—BLESSINGS IN THE TEMPLE—JOURNEY TO SALT LAKE VALLEY.

ON the 11th of November, while still a prisoner of war, I was married, which might be considered as a proof that I had not lost hope. I was fortunate in securing a wife who was zealous and devoted to her religion and ready to sacrifice or endure anything to further its interests.

After the troops were withdrawn from Far West I visited my farm two miles south of the town, to look after my stock which I had left there, and found that all my earthly possessions save my real estate had been confiscated by the army.

On visiting the late camp-ground of the army I found the heads of eleven of my oxen which had been butchered, and there was no trace left of my sheep, swine, etc.

Brother John Butler, who had been obliged to flee to the north to save his life, had left his family in my charge. He had a span of very poor horses and an old wagon. I loaded the wagon up with his wife and five children and what few goods I had left, which consisted of one trunk full of clothes besides what my wife and I wore. I managed to find one of my horses which the mob had taken and used in such a shocking manner that his back was skinned almost from his withers to his tail. This animal I hitched on ahead of Brother Butler's horses, and by those of us walking who were able to do so, we slowly made our way to Quincy, Illinois, in the depth of winter. On arriving there I went to work carrying the hod up a four-story building—really the first hard work I had ever done, to make another start in life, while my wife assisted by taking in sewing.

In the month of July I removed to Montrose, opposite Commerce. In May of the following year I went on a mission to Tennessee, from which I returned the following October, and again the next year, I went to Charleston, South Carolina, being instructed to introduce the gospel there. I spent all the money I had in renting halls and publishing placards announcing my meetings, but although I had large audiences, and numbers of persons came to me, Nicodemus-like—by night, to inquire about the gospel, I failed to make one convert. I returned to Nauvoo from this mission in 1842.

In the summer of 1843, I took a trip through southern Illinois and north-western Kentucky, in the interest of the Nauvoo House, and in May, 1844, I again went south to Tennessee to electioneer for Joseph Smith as candidate for the Presidency of the United States. On arriving at Dresden, Tenn., I rented the court-house to hold meeting in, and while in the act of preaching to a good-sized audience, a mob gathered outside and a shot was fired at me through the window. The bullet passed near my head and lodged in the ceiling, and immediately afterwards a few brickbats were also thrown through the window. Considerable excitement followed and the audience began to scatter, when a man by the name of Camp, somewhat noted as a fighting character, arose and called on the fleeing people to stop. He told them if they would only sit and listen to the preaching, he would go out and look after the persons who were creating the disturbance. About two-thirds of the audience again became seated and he went outside and procured a shot-gun, with which he patroled around the court-house the remainder of the evening, and there was no further trouble.

Another meeting was announced for the following day, but before it commenced a lawyer of the town laid his plans to break it up. I had not long been speaking when he, at the head of a mob of two hundred men, marched into the room and demanded that I should cease speaking, as they had come to attend to my case.

In this emergency, and for the only time in my life in public, I made use of a masonic sign calling for help, when lo! a number of persons sprang up to assist me. The lawyer was commanded to give his reasons for interfering with me, which he proceeded to do by delivering a most abusive and slanderous speech. I finally commanded him to sit down and he did so very suddenly, and the masons who were present, who were very numerous and influential, gave him to understand that he would not be allowed to molest me. I continued my remarks, and at the close of the meeting Mr. Camp took vengeance on the lawyer by knocking him down and kicking him around the court-house yard.

From Dresden I proceeded to Paris, in the same State, where I contracted for the publication of 1,000 copies of Joseph Smith's "Powers and Policy of the Government of the United States." After the printing had been done and paid for, the printer informed me that if I attempted to circulate the pamphlets it would be likely to land me in the penitentiary, as the views expressed therein, in regard to freeing the slaves, would be considered treasonable and contrary to law. On consulting a lawyer of the place, a boyhood friend of mine, I found that he held the same opinion, and I therefore suppressed the whole edition.

I was at Father Church's, on Duck river, in Hickman Co., Tenn., when I received the news of the martyrdom of Joseph and Hyrum Smith, six days after the consummation of that bloody deed. I immediately proceeded down Duck river to the Tennessee river, by canoe, and, on arriving there, in company with three other Elders, purchased a skiff, and made my way to Paducah on the Ohio river, from which place I took steamer to Nauvoo.

On arriving in Nauvoo I found that Sidney Rigdon was striving to establish his claim to the leadership of the Church, and proffering various unheard-of offices to such persons as would rally around his standard. However, on the arrival of President Young and the other Apostles from their missions, his claims were soon set aside.

I was present at the meeting held in Nauvoo on the occasion when President Young assumed the leadership of the Church, and can testify with hundreds of others that he spoke by the power of God on that occasion and that he had the very voice and appearance of Joseph Smith.

The following autumn I was sent by President Young to Kentucky, Tennessee, Alabama, Georgia and Mississippi to raise means for the building of the Temple and also to induce the Saints scattered through that region to migrate to Nauvoo and make preparations to journey westward. I returned to Nauvoo in the summer of 1845, bringing a large number of the Saints with me. I also left many others partially prepared to follow, who were subsequently gathered up by Elders John Brown and Wm. Crosby and led westward, by way of Arkansas, to Salt Lake Valley.

After my return to Nauvoo I labored on the Temple until it was so far completed as to admit of the ordinances being performed in it, when I had the blessed privilege of entering it and receiving my endowments and having wives sealed to me. I also at that time had the son of my first wife (who, I should have mentioned, was a widow when I married her) adopted to me by the Priesthood, and he has ever since borne my name and been recognized and treated as one of my own sons.

I labored about three months in the temple in administering the ordinances of the house of God to others, and in April, 1846, I left Nauvoo and started westward with quite a large company of my southern friends. On arriving at Winter Quarters I was ordained a Bishop and appointed to preside over a Ward, and spent the winter in building cabins to shelter the people and in looking after the wants of the poor. In the spring of 1847 I was appointed to organize and lead westward a company of Saints having one hundred and twenty wagons. I chose as my assistants Major Russell and Geo. B. Wallace. We arrived in Salt Lake Valley on the 24th day of September.

Thus passed the first twelve years of my connection with the Church—twelve years of rough but not unprofitable experience for me, considering the many lessons I learned and the satisfaction I enjoyed in contemplating my labors. During that period I had become strong and healthy, and through the blessings of God, had been enabled, with the help of my wife and boy, to earn a subsistence and accumulate some property, notwithstanding the many missions I had filled and the losses of property I had sustained.

Since that time I never have performed a regular preaching mission abroad, although in 1851, I was sent to England, for that purpose; but on arriving there it was decided to have me return to lead the first company emigrated by the Perpetual Emigration Fund across the plains, and after a stay of thirty days in that country I did so. I filled various business missions, however, in which I crossed the plains thirteen times with ox and mule teams.

CHAPTER III.

ALMOST LOST IN THE ATLANTIC—NARROWLY ESCAPE THE "SALUDA" DISASTER—NEARLY DEAD WITH THE CHOLERA—HEALED IN ANSWER TO PRAYER—BLOWN UP WITH A KEG OF POWDER—A SICK WOMAN HEALED—ELDER PATTEN'S REMARKABLE PREDICTION FULFILLED—A MAN ALMOST DEAD RECOVERS ON BEING BAPTIZED.

DURING my experience I have seen the power of God manifested upon various occasions in preserving my life; indeed, considering the many narrow escapes I have had, it might be almost thought that I have had a charmed life.

On my return from England in 1853, on board the new steamer *Pacific*, we encountered a severe storm, in which the deck was swept clear of rigging, the deck cabin, one of the wheels, both wheel houses and the bulwarks. The steamer was entirely submerged in the sea at one time, and had she not been very well built she would never have come to the surface again. It looked like a precarious time, but I felt an assurance that the vessel would be saved, and in the midst of all the excitement which prevailed among the crew and passengers I felt quite calm. I had seventeen thousand dollars in gold in my possession, and I did not even fear that I would lose that. Our preservation, however, was certainly providential, for the vessel was in a terribly dilapidated condition, but we finally arrived safely in New York with the wrecked vessel, after a voyage of sixteen days.

I subsequently had a very narrow escape on the occasion of the *Saluda* disaster. I had purchased the supplies for my company to make its overland journey with, except cattle, at St. Louis, and had decided to go farther up the river to buy the stock, when Eli B. Kelsey came to me to consult me in regard to chartering the *Saluda* to convey an independent company of Saints up the river. I went with him to examine the boat, and on finding that it was an old hulk of a freight boat, fitted up with a single engine, I strongly advised him against having anything to do with it. He seemed to be influenced in making choice of it entirely by the fact that he could get it cheaper than a better one; but in my opinion it seemed folly, for in addition to the danger of accident, the length of time likely to be occupied in making the journey would more than counterbalance what might be saved in the charge for transit. However, he decided to charter it, and then both he and the captain urged me strongly to take passage with them, offering to carry me free of cost if I would only go, but I could not feel satisfied to do so. I followed a few days afterwards on the *Isabella*, and overtook them at Lexington, where the *Saluda* was stopped by the float-ice and was unable to proceed farther. I went on board of her to visit the Saints (who were in charge of D. J. Ross, Eli B. Kelsey having gone ashore to purchase cattle), and left just before the last plank was drawn in, preparatory to attempting to start. I had not walked to exceed two hundred yards after leaving the *Saluda* before the explosion occurred, and on turning to look in the direction of the the ill-fated boat I saw the bodies of many of the unfortunate passengers and various parts of the boat flying in the air in every direction. Fortunately for the Saints on board, they were mostly on the deck of the boat and pretty well towards the stern, and they consequently fared better than those who were below, or on the forepart of the boat, which was blown entirely to pieces. As it was, however, upwards of twenty of the Saints were lost or subsequently died of their wounds. My own preservation I can only attribute to the providence of the Almighty, for if I had remained a moment on the wharf to see the boat start, as would have been very natural for a person to do, I would have been blown into eternity as those were who stood there.

I shall never forget the kindness of the citizens of Lexington in caring for the living and burying the dead. The Lord certainly inspired them to do all that sympathy and benevolence could suggest in aid of the afflicted. The city council set apart a piece of ground in which to bury the Saints who had died, and William H. Russell, the great government freighter, and many other prominent citizens did all they could to comfort and help the afflicted survivors. Besides their devoted attention, their contributions in aid of the Saints amounted to thousands of dollars.

The disaster described is really the only accident of any consequence by water that has befallen a company of Latter-day Saints in emigrating from the old countries, and there was much reason to believe that Providence was in their favor to a great extent even in that case, or a much greater number would certainly have lost their lives.

I remained at Lexington about eight days looking after the interests of the Saints and purchasing stock, after which I returned to St. Louis, where I met the company of Saints I was to conduct across the plains. On reaching Atchison, our starting point for the overland journey, the company was stricken with the cholera. There were over forty cases, and of these some fifteen proved fatal. Numbers were healed instantaneously through the prayer of faith when the Elders laid their hands upon them, although apparently near death's door; others gave way entirely to fear, failed to exercise faith and soon died. After we had started upon our journey and when the last person who had been afflicted had recovered, I was prostrated with the same dread disease. The train was stopped and the whole company fasted and prayed for two days for my recovery, but I continued growing worse until my limbs and the lower portion of my body were apparently dead, but then the faith of the Saints and the power of the Almighty prevailed in my behalf and I recovered. I had, however, lost seventy-five pounds in weight within a few days.

Another remarkable instance in which the providence of the the Almighty was manifest in my preservation occurred in the following May. I was emptying a small keg of powder and standing in a stooping position right over it, and as it did not run out very freely I shook the keg, when it exploded. The staves and pieces of hoops were scattered in every direction, some pieces being afterwards found at least eight rods distant. I was blown into the air and my face and hands most terribly burned. It was a marvel that the staves of the keg were not driven through my body, but it did not appear that a single one had struck me. The whole of the skin came from my face and hands, yet, wonderful to relate, there is not now a mark of powder about my face, and my eyesight, the loss of which I was most fearful of, was not at all impaired by it.

This series of narrow escapes which I have related I passed through within a little over a year; and it really seemed to me that Satan was bent upon my destruction. The fact that my life was preserved through them was an evidence to me of the power of God and that He had a purpose in allowing me to live.

I have witnessed the power of God displayed in the healing of persons who were sick in hundreds of instances, in some cases that would probably be considered by the world as very wonderful, but to which the Saints, whose experience has been similar to my own, had become accustomed. I think Elder David W. Patten possessed the gift of healing to a greater degree than any man I ever associated with. I remember on one occasion when I was laboring with him as a missionary in Tennessee, he was sent for to administer to a woman who had been sick for five years and bed-ridden for one year and not able to help herself. Brother Patten stepped to her bedside and asked her if she believed in the Lord Jesus Christ. She replied that she did. He then took her by the hand and said, "In the name of Jesus Christ, arise!"

She immediately sat up in bed, when he placed his hands upon her head and rebuked her disease, pronounced blessings upon her head and promised that she should bear children. She had been married for seven years and had never had any children, and this promise seemed very unlikely ever to be fulfilled. But she arose from her bed immediately, walked half a mile to be baptized and back again in her wet clothes. She was healed from that time, and within one year became a mother, and afterwards bore several children.

I was myself healed under his administration in a manner which appeared to me very remarkable at that time. While traveling I was taken very sick and was forced to seek entertainment at the house of an infidel. Elder Patten was desirous of administering to me and, by way of a pretext, asked the privilege of praying. His request was granted and he knelt beside the bed upon which I was lying, and, without the family noticing it, placed his hand upon my head. While his hand was upon me, I felt the disease pass off from my system as palpably as I ever experienced anything in my life, and before he arose from his knees I was as well as I ever had been, and able to arise and eat my supper.

I remember a rather remarkable instance of healing that occurred at Winter Quarters, which I think worth relating:

During the winter of 1846-7 while the Saints were encamped on the banks of the Missouri there was a great deal of sickness among them, and many died. Among others who were afflicted was a man by the name of Collins, who had followed up the Church for some time on account of his wife being a member, but who never felt quite satisfied to embrace the gospel, although he never opposed the work. When he was taken sick it was not thought by his friends that he could recover, as he had appeared to be sinking rapidly under the effects of the disease, and for some time he lay in a semi-unconscious state, from which it was feared he would never rally.

However, he finally regained consciousness and looked around, when I asked him if he had any message to leave before he died. He immediately replied that it would not do for him to die then, as he had not been baptized, and urged very strongly to be taken right down to the river to receive this ordinance.

Yielding to his solicitations, some of the brethren brought the running gear of a wagon with a few boards on it, up to the door of the cabin in which he was living, and his bed, with him lying upon it, was carried out and placed on the wagon. When we had proceeded part way down to the river the wagon tire commenced running off one of the wheels and a halt was made to hammer it on again. On noticing the wagon stop and hearing the hammering, he inquired what was the matter, and when he was informed that the tire was running off, he replied impatiently, "Oh, never mind the tire; go on, or I'll die and go to hell yet before I'm baptized!"

We proceeded on with him till we reached the river, which at that time was frozen over, but the ice had been cut away near the shore in order that our animals might drink. There he was lifted from his bed, carried into the water and I baptized him for the remission of his sins and his restoration to health. After being taken out of the water a blanket was wrapped around him and he was seated for a moment to rest upon a block of ice upon the shore. Seeing the brethren turning the wagon around, he inquired what they were going to do. They replied that they were going to put him on the bed and haul him back home, when he arose to his feet and assured them that they need not go to that trouble, for he could walk back, and he did so, and from that time became a healthy man.

SCENES IN THE BRITISH MISSION.

CHAPTER I.

ELDER HALLIDAY APPLIED TO FOR HELP BY A SISTER WHOSE SON IS DYING—NOT ABLE TO GO, HE GAVE THE LADY HIS HANDKERCHIEF AND PROMISES HER THE CHILD SHALL LIVE—THE CHILD REVIVES FROM APPARENT DEATH BY THE WOMAN'S FAITH AND PRAYER—PREACHING IN PENZANCE—DISCOURAGEMENT AND WANT—STRANGE CONDUCT OF A LADY ATTENDING THE MEETING—INVITATION TO GO TO ST. JUST—GIFT OF TONGUES AND INTERPRETATION GIVEN TO ELDER HALLIDAY, THROUGH WHICH HE RECEIVES A REVELATION—REVELATION LITERALLY FULFILLED.

THE various gifts of the gospel were perhaps enjoyed to as great an extent by the Elders who labored in England in an early day as they have been by any people and in any place, at least in this dispensation. Nor were the manifestations of these gifts confined to the Elders who were engaged in the ministry, for their converts also enjoyed them to a very great extent. Many of them through their extraordinary faith and humility called forth the blessings and power of God in various ways. The gift of healing was very manifest, and scores of instances might be related wherein persons were healed in a most miraculous manner.

Bishop George Halliday, of Santaquin, who labored extensively as a missionary in his native country in an early day, relates an incident of this kind. Upon a warm Sunday evening, after he had been preaching to an audience in Bristol, he was accosted by a Mrs. Ware, a sister in the Church, who told him she had a son extremely sick and thought to be dying. She begged him to go home with her and administer to it. She lived three miles distant, on Durham Down. It was quite late in the evening and he was so extremely tired that he scarcely felt able to comply with her request; and yet he did not like to decline. All at once he felt impressed to say: "Here, Sister Ware, you take my handkerchief and go home to your child and lay it on him wherever he seems to be affected, praying to the Lord to heal him. If you do this I will promise you that he will recover."

With full faith the good lady took the handkerchief and departed. On reaching her home she was met at the door by her daughters and friends, who informed her that her son was dead.

"No," said she, "I cannot believe it! Brother Halliday has promised me that he shall live, and I have his handkerchief to lay upon him."

She hastened to the boy and did as she had been directed to, and the child, which a few minutes before had been inanimate, began to show signs of life. The next morning he was able to come down to breakfast, and soon regained his wonted health. He afterwards emigrated to Utah.

Brother Halliday also relates another instance in which the power of God was displayed in a rather remarkable manner, near the same time:

He and Elder John Chislett were sent to Penzance, Cornwall, to introduce the gospel to the inhabitants. They met with no encouragement, yet they did not feel justified in leaving the place until they had given the people a thorough warning. Their funds were so low that the two of them were forced to live on a penny's worth of bread and a penny's worth of soup per day; yet their faith was strong, and they spent much of their time in prayer. Finally, as a last resort, in the effort to awaken an interest in the message they had to bear to the people, they decided to give a course of public lectures. Elder Halliday pawned his watch to raise the necessary money to rent a hall and publish some placards announcing their meetings, and on the first evening appointed they were gratified at seeing a few come to hear them. Among the audience they noticed particularly a well-dressed gentleman and lady, the latter of whom commenced weeping almost as soon as she entered the hall and continued to do so as long as the meeting lasted. The Elders, of course, could assign no reason for this peculiar conduct while the meeting was in progress, nor were they any more enlightened when, at the close of the services, the lady came forward with her husband and invited them to visit her at her home at St. Just, about six miles distant. This was the first invitation they had received from anyone in the place, and they accepted it joyfully, and would willingly have gone home with her that night, but, to their disappointment, she named the following Wednesday as the time when she would be pleased to receive them. Nothing further passed between them, but it was evident that a favorable impression had been made upon her, and that she was a woman of intelligence and refinement. While anticipating the pleasure of visiting her and waiting for the day to arrive, the Elders continued to subsist upon their scanty fare, and spent their time in vainly endeavoring to proselyte among the citizens of Penzance.

Wednesday morning came and with it a drenching rain storm, through which the Elders tramped the whole six miles, hungry and penniless. Shortly before arriving at St. Just, and while they were crossing a plowed field, with the mud clinging to their boots so they could scarcely walk, the Lord deigned to comfort them by giving Elder Halliday the gift of tongues and the interpretation of the same, in which it was made known to him that the lady whom they were going to visit had been favored with a vision in which she had seen himself and Elder Chislett; also that she was the owner of several houses, one of which she was going to allow them to use to hold meetings in, and that he was going to baptize her that very night.

As soon as this had passed through his mind, for he had not spoken aloud, but to himself, he joyfully slapped his companion on the shoulder and exclaimed, "Cheer up, John! I have had a revelation!" He then proceeded to relate all that had been revealed to him.

When they arrived at the house they were drenched as badly as if they had been in a river. Even their boots were full of water, so that when they pulled them off and turned the tops downward it ran out of them in a stream. Their friend, however, had been anxiously looking for them, and had prepared a blazing fire to warm them and spread the table with tempting food. She also proposed for them to change their clothes as far as she could supply them with dry ones to put on from her husband's wardrobe. "But," said she, "I can hardly wait for you to change your clothes, I am so anxious to talk to you."

"Oh, you need not be in such a hurry," remarked Elder Halliday, 'for I know what you are going to say!"

She looked at him in surprise and inquired how he knew.

"Why," he said, "I have had it revealed to me on the way here." He then related to her every particular as it had been made known to him, until he got to that part relating to her baptism, when she interrupted him by exclaiming in surprise to her husband:

"There, now, is that not just as it occurred? How could he have learned that? for you know I have not talked with anyone but you about it!" She then admitted that the week previous, while lying awake in bed, she saw a bright light in the room and awoke her husband and pointed it out to him. He also saw it, and it passed around the room in the direction of Penzance, to which place it led her in her mind, and there she saw two men trying to raise a standard, in which labor the people who looked on seemed unwilling to lend a helping hand. She reproached them for their lack of interest, and took hold herself to assist. This vision was so plain that she afterwards related the whole of it to her husband and even described the appearance of the men. Then she could not rest until she had, in company with her husband, visited Penzance and attended the lecture she there saw announced. As soon as she entered the hall and saw the two Elders she recognized them and could not refrain from crying. As to the other part of what had been revealed to him, she said it was true that she was the owner of a row of houses, which she pointed out to the Elders, and that the last one was a school-house in which her husband taught school, and which they were welcome to use as a meeting house as long as they wanted to free of charge.

"But," said Elder Halliday, "that is not all that the Lord revealed to me. He told me that I was going to baptize you before I went to bed to-night, and now I want your husband to go and find some water for that purpose."

Brother Halliday, in telling what had been revealed to him, felt a good deal as he imagined the prophet Jonah must have felt when the Lord commanded him to go to Nineveh and declare the destruction of that city. He had before him the fear of being declared a false prophet, and it required a great deal of faith in him to tell it, especially that part relating to her baptism. However, he was soon relieved on that score, for the good lady expressed her readiness and anxiety to go immediately and be baptized. But her husband declared there was not a stream or pond in that region deep enough to baptize a person in, and it would be no use for them to think of doing such a thing that day. "Is there not a ditch or hollow anywhere around here that is deep enough?" said Elder Halliday, "Please go and see."

The husband complied with a dubious look on his face, while the Elders proceeded to change and dry their clothes, and soon he returned and reported that the heavy shower which had fallen had so filled all the ditches and low places that they would have no difficulty in finding water deep enough.

Within two hours from the arrival of the Elders the lady was baptized and confirmed, she being the first one to embrace the gospel in the region known as "Land's End."

The Elders ever found a home at her house and enjoyed the privilege of holding meetings in her school-house for years, and she remained faithful, but her husband, although he was kind to the Elders and willing to entertain them, never joined the Church. He was an infidel and an astrologer.

CHAPTER II.

ELDER ELIAS MORRIS FALLS WITH A SCAFFOLD A DISTANCE OF THIRTY FEET WITHOUT BEING HURT—GIFT OF HEALING POSSESSED BY ELDER ABEL EVANS—A WOMAN HEALED WHO HAD HER FACE EATEN AWAY BY A CANCER—STORM AT SEA REBUKED—A BROKEN LEG CURED—A BROKEN SKULL MENDED—FEVER ON SHIPBOARD STOPPED BY THE PRAYER OF FAITH.

ELDER Elias Morris, now a resident of Salt Lake City, labored extensively as a local and traveling Elder in the Welch mission in an early day. In illustration of the manner in which the Lord's power was often manifested in preserving the lives of His servants, he relates an instance from his experience:

While acting as a local Elder in his native place, laboring at his trade during the week and preaching in the surrounding villages on Sundays, he once had occasion to speak of the signs which the Savior had promised should follow believers: "In my name they shall cast out devils; they shall speak with new tongues; they shall take up serpents; and if they drink any deadly, thing it shall not hurt them; they shall lay hands on the sick, and they shall recover." He argued that the enjoyment of those promised blessings was not limited to the believers who lived when the Savior was upon the earth, but that the faithful Latter-day Saints also shared the same. The sectarian preachers of the neighborhood who listened to or heard of Elder Morris' remarks on that occasion ridiculed them, and one especially, a Methodist deacon, had a great deal to say about them. In repeating those remarks and commenting on them to others, he also exaggera‘ed what had been said, even asserting falsely that Elder Morris had claimed that if he were to fall from the top of a quarry it would not hurt

A FALL OF THIRTY FEET WITHOUT INJURY.

him. Elder Morris heard of this deacon's exaggerated stories and flippant comments, but did not deign to notice them, although he was well acquainted with the man, in fact he was at that very time in his employ.

A few days afterwards Elder Morris happened to be engaged upon a three-story building, pointing the front, and for that purpose was sitting on a hanging scaffold near the top of the wall. All at once he felt the scaffold giving way, the planks upon which it rested, and which projected from the inside of the building, having become loosened. He called immediately to a fellow workman engaged inside the building to come to his relief, but before the man reached the window to grasp the plank, the scaffold fell and Brother Morris with it. With a silent prayer to God for help, and fully realizing his danger, he dropped the distance of thirty feet or more, alighting on his thigh on the stone pavement. In an instant he was upon his feet, and placing his hand on a window sill, he sprang lightly into the lower room of the building and escaped the falling planks, which did not reach the ground until after he had, and came forth the next minute unharmed. He did not even feel the slightest pain from the fall.

It happened that the Methodist deacon, one of the owners of the building, and Elder Morris' father were in the street in front of the building at the time of the accident, and the latter was almost paralyzed with fear at the sight of his boy falling down, and no less surprised and overjoyed at seeing him walk forth the next moment unscathed. The deacon, too, seemed very much astonished and hardly able to believe the evidence of his own sight when he saw the man whose religious pretentions he had ridiculed so much pass through such an ordeal and appear unhurt. Elder Morris noticed his surprised look as he approached him, and thought it a fitting opportunity to tax him with the slander and ridicule which he had been indulging in at his expense. He accordingly did so, and then asked ironically, hinting at the story which the deacon had circulated about him, "Isn't that almost equal to falling off a quarry?" The deacon acknowledged that it was, and declared that some supernatural power must have saved him in that instance at least.

Many anecdotes are related of Elder Abel Evans, formerly of Lehi, in this Territory, who died while on a mission in Wales some years since. He was a man of wonderful faith, and possessed the gift of healing in a remarkable degree. While laboring as a missionary in Wales in an early day he met a sister who was a member of the Church and was afflicted with a terrible cancer in her face which had eaten away her upper lip and the greater portion of her nose. She had tried all the doctors she could find who pretended to cure cancers and they had one after another given her case up as hopeless. When Brother Evans met her she was mourning over her affliction and recounting her suffering and the efforts she had made to get relief. He listened to her story and then asked: "Why do you not apply to the Great Physician to cure you?"

"Do you think it would be of any use?" she asked, brightening up.

"Why," he replied "with the Lord all things are possible! If you have faith you can be healed!"

She expressed her anxiety to be administered to, and he forthwith purchased a bottle of olive oil, consecrated it and anointed her face, applying the oil with a feather to the worst part. He also rebuked the disease and prayed for her recovery, and from that hour the cancer was killed and her face began to heal. He repeated the operation two or three times, and, strange as it may appear, the flesh and skin actually grew again upon that part of her face which had been eaten away and a new nose in time developed—not a perfect one it is true, but one that was a great improvement upon none at all. Notwithstanding this great manifestation of God's goodness to her, however, this woman afterwards apostatized.

On one occaison Brother Evans was sailing from Liverpool to Bangor, at which place he had an appointment to preach, when a terrible storm arose, which threatened the destruction of the vessel. When the officers and crew were all ready to give up hope, Elder Evans retired to a secluded part of the vessel, called upon the Lord in prayer, reminding Him of the appointment to be filled and that he was upon His business, and, in mighty faith, rebuked the storm, when it calmed so suddenly that all hands on board were as much surprised as delighted, and quite at a loss to account for the sudden change in their prospects.

In the year 1846, a man living in Merthyr Tydvil, who was a member of the Church, happened accidentally to break his leg between the knee and ankle. A surgeon was called in, who set the broken bones, bound the limb up with bandages and splints and cautioned the patient to keep perfectly quiet until the fracture could have time to knit. Three days afterwards Elders Abel Evans and Thomas D. Giles called to see him, and the former questioned him as to his faith. "Do you believe," said he, "that the Lord has power to heal your broken limb?"

The man acknowledged that he did.

"Do you believe," he again asked, "that we, as the servants of God, holding the Priesthood, have authority to call upon the Almighty and claim a blessing for you at His hands?"

The man assured him that he did.

"Then," said he, "If you wish it we will take the bandages off your broken leg and anoint it."

The man consented, the bandages and splints were removed and his leg was anointed with consecrated oil. The brethren then placed their hands upon his head, and Elder Evans rebuked the power of the evil one, commanded the bones to come together and knit, and, finally, that the man should arise from his bed and walk. He got out of bed immediately and walked about the house, and from that time had no occasion to use a bandage on the injured limb or even walk with a stick.

While crossing the sea in 1850, emigrating to Utah, a number of remarkable cases of healing occurred under his administration. One was that of a young girl who was terribly afflicted with evil spirits, and who was entirely relieved when he placed his hands upon her head. Another was that of a little boy who fell through the hatchway of the vessel, alighting upon his head on the ring and bolt of the lower hatchway. When he was picked up it was found that the force of the fall had driven the iron upon which he struck into his head, and within a minute afterwards the injured place puffed up like a distended bladder. Of course, he was knocked insensible and apparently lifeless, but Brother Evans and one or two other

Elders immediately administered to him, and while their hands were upon his head the swelling entirely disappeared and he was restored to consciousness and to health. This was witnessed and marveled at by a number of persons who were not in the Church as well as a great many of the Saints who were on board.

When Elder Evans was crossing the Atlantic in charge of a company of Saints emigrating to Utah, a terrible epidemic in the nature of a fever broke out on the ship, and threatened the destruction of all on board. He felt that their only hope lay in securing the favor of the Almighty, and determined to muster all the faith he could in appealing to the Lord. He called together four Elders of experience who were on board, and asked them to retire with him to the hold of the vessel and unite in prayer. They did so again and again without any apparent good result, and Brother Evans marveled at the cause. It was such an unusual thing for him to fail to have his prayers answered, that he was surprised that it should be so in that instance, and he could only account for it by lack of union or worthiness on the part of the Elders. He therefore called the four Elders again to retire with him to the hold of the ship, and took with him a basin of clean water. When they had reached a secluded place where they were not likely to be overheard or disturbed by others, he talked to the Elders about the necessity of their being united in faith and clear of sin before God if they desired to call upon Him and receive a blessing. "Now," he said, "I want each of you Elders, who feels that his conscience is clear before God, who has committed no sin to debar him from the enjoyment of the Holy Spirit, and who has faith in the Lord Jesus Christ sufficient to call upon the Almighty in His name and claim the desired blessing, to wash his hands in that basin!" Three of the Elders stepped forward and did so; the fourth could not—his conscience smote him. He was therefore asked kindly to retire, and the four others joined in earnest prayer before the Lord and rebuked the disease by which the people were afflicted. The result was that the epidemic ceased its ravages and the sick recovered from that very hour, much to the surprise of the ship's officers and others on board who knew nothing of the power by which such a happy result was accomplished.

NUMEROUS PERSONS HEALED.

In the winter of 1850, Elder Abel Evans lived at Council Bluffs, on the eastern bank of the Missouri river. A great many of the Saints were there at the time working for an outfit for their overland journey or awaiting the return of fine weather before starting across the plains. That locality was somewhat noted for its insalubriety, but during that winter an unusually large amount of sickness prevailed. Some of the more prominent Elders were kept quite busy going about from house to house administering to the sick among the Saints, and scores, perhaps hundreds of cases of healing occurred under their hands, many of which were quite remarkable. Sister Ashton, now of Salt Lake City, relates how she was healed there when near death's door, and under circumstances the memory of which even now causes her to shed tears. She had been sick for a considerable length of time and so bad for two weeks that she had not been able to take a mouthful of food, when she heard of the death of her father.

In her weak condition this intelligence was a heavy blow to her. Her mother had died previously and been buried without her having the privilege of being with her during her sickness or even seeing her face when dead, and the thought of being deprived of this privilege in the case of her father also, almost overcame her. She had during her sickness felt a strong desire to live, and now in addition to that she was anxious to see her dead father before he was buried, and attend his funeral. Some of the Elders came and administered to her, but they were not men in whom she had a great deal of faith, and she failed to receive any benefit from their administration. After awhile, however, Brother Evans called to see her, and, on learning of her desire to attend her father's funeral, he promised her without any hesitation that she would do so. Placing his hands upon her head, he rebuked the sickness with which she was prostrated and pronounced the blessing of health upon her. She arose immediately from her bed, and rode six miles that same day, and saw her father buried.

CHAPTER III.

ELDER JOHN PARRY'S STATEMENT—HIS BROTHER'S TESTIMONY AND DEATH—HIS SISTER'S REPROOF AND DEATH—EMBRACE THE GOSPEL—HIS SLEEP TROUBLED—A REMEDY AND A LESSON—ORSON SPENCER HEALED—PROVIDENTIAL HELP—ESCAPE FROM A MOB—CANCER IN A MAN'S FACE CURED BY LAYING ON OF HANDS—PRESERVED FROM MOBS.

ELDER JOHN PARRY, who was master-mason on the Logan Temple up to the time of his death, which occurred in July last, left a manuscript journal in which a number of very interesting incidents are recorded.

His brother, Bernard Parry, died on the 12th of November, 1841, while a member of the Campbellite church, and without having heard of the gospel as revealed through Joseph Smith. While upon his death bed, however, his mind was illumined by the Spirit of God and he had the gift of prophecy. He said that the Lord had shown him many great and marvelous things which were to come to pass in this age, but that he would not live to see them, for he was about to die. "But," said he, addressing his father, "the Lord is going to do a great work and a wonder upon the earth, and you shall be called to take part in it, father; and you shall yet preach the everlasting gospel to thousands in Wales."

Then turning to his brother John, he said, "And you also, John, shall be called to it, and shall preach the gospel to tens of thousands, and shall baptize many, and my body shall not altogether rot before the Savior will stand upon the earth."

The night before he died, he inquired of his brother John if he would be willing to do just as he requested him. John replied that he would, when he asked him to remove the things, one by one, that stood upon a table near by, into another room. His brother complied without saying a word, and was then requested to return them and arrange them as they were before upon the table. This John also did without asking a question, whereupon Bernard said, "Well done; now I wish you to remember that that is the way to serve the Lord! whatever He commands you to do, do it without asking questions."

After impressing this lesson upon his brother's mind, he lay back upon his pillow and never spoke again.

Elder Parry never heard the gospel preached until five years after his brother's death, but the prediction in regard to his preaching and baptizing was literally fulfilled.

A sister of his also had peculiar impressions before her death, which occurred about five years later. She had, while living in Cheltenham some time previously, met some Latter-day Saints, and become somewhat acquainted with the doctrines which they preached. On returning to the parental home she frequently referred to these doctrines, and urged her relatives to investigate them, but her father and her brother John, who were zealous Campbellites, were prejudiced against the "Mormons" by the false reports which they had heard about them and opposed her and persuaded her to have nothing to do with them.

She was taken sick with a fever, and when about to die she called her relatives around her and said to her father, "Your religion is worth nothing in the hour of death. I have lived it as faithfully as mortal could do, and it is of no good to me now. I am going to utter darkness, therefore look to yourselves and seek a religion that will support you and enable you to face death fearlessly—the one that you have is of no value!"

Then turning to her brother John, she reproached him with having hindered and persuaded her from embracing the gospel of Jesus Christ.

This was too much for him to bear, for he loved his sister dearly, and he fainted and fell to the floor. When he regained his consciousness his sister had ceased speaking and soon died.

Brother Parry gives an account of the manner in which he became acquainted with the Latter-day Saints and embraced the gospel.

In 1844, a friend of his told him that Joseph Smith, the Prophet had been killed. As soon as he heard this, something whispered to him: "He was a servant of God." From that moment his prejudice against the Latter-day Saints was removed.

He heard but little of "Mormonism" after that until he removed to Birkenhead, in 1846. While going from there to Liverpool in company with some of his relatives and friends, he met a "Mormon" Elder, who invited him to attend one of their meetings to be held in the last named place. He persuaded his companions to accompany him, and they all attended the meeting. While listening to the Elders bear their testimony to the great latter-day work, he felt convinced that they spoke the truth, and believed them with all his heart.

At the close of the meeting, he asked one of his friends, a Campbellite preacher, what he thought of the "Mormons" and their doctrines. The preacher replied that their doctrines were a "damnable heresy."

"Well," said Mr. Parry, "one of the sayings of Paul has been fulfilled with you and me to-day."

"What is that?" asked the preacher.

"When he said the gospel would be unto one 'the savor of death unto death: and to the other the savor of life unto life.' It has been life unto life to me, and I shall be a Latter-day Saint," was the response.

He attended another meeting in the evening of the same day, and at the close he and his father handed in their names for baptism.

Shortly after he was baptized Brother Parry was ordained an Elder and was appointed to preside over the Birkenhead branch of the Church. While praying subsequently for a testimony of the truth, a voice spoke to him and said: "The gift of healing shall follow thee to a great extent."

This was literally fulfilled.

After joining the Church Elder Parry was often troubled in his sleep by evil spirits. Upon one occasion he inquired of the president of the Liverpool branch why it was that he was thus annoyed. The Elder replied that some persons were troubled more than others, and told him to use the following words in his prayers before retiring to rest: "O God, the Eternal Father, I ask Thee in the name of Thy Son, Jesus Christ, to give Thine angels charge concerning me this night, and allow not the powers of darkness to molest my spirit nor body."

He did this, and was troubled with evil spirits no more, until one night, feeling very sleepy, he uttered a hasty, formal prayer and went to bed. During the night he was almost overcome by the power of evil spirits, which were visible. Unable to utter a word, he prayed fervently in his mind to the Lord to release him. In an instant the heavens appeared to him to open, and he saw an angel descend towards him. The personage took hold of him and raised him up a little, and immediately the powers of darkness disappeared.

Elder Parry asked the angel why it was that the Lord permitted the evil one to abuse him in such a manner, to which he replied: "Because thou didst not pray from the heart, but with thy lips."

At one time Elder Orson Spencer came from Liverpool to spend a few days at a place where Elder Parry was living. While there he was taken very sick. Elder Parry anointed him and he soon recovered.

A short time after this the Birkenhead branch of the Church was disorganized, and Elder Parry was sent to Wales to preach. He was soon out of money, and being without a place to stop, he and his fellow-laborer took lodgings in a small store. They called for food on credit, trusting the Lord would provide means to enable them to pay their way. The next day they held two meetings, and enough money was given them to pay for their board and some to help them in their travels.

Upon another occasion, he was obliged to put up at a boarding house, as he was a stranger in the place, and there were none who would entertain him. He had no money with which to pay his board when he went there, but after holding a meeting and telling the people that he was a stranger, without money, and was sent to preach without purse or scrip, several of the congregation donated small sums to help him. While on his way to the house where he was stopping, a child came to him from the opposite side of the street and placed in his hand a half-penny. When he went to settle for his board and lodgings he found that he had just the exact amount with which he was charged.

While holding a meeting in the open air, at one time, Elder Parry and another traveling Elder were disturbed by a ruffian who challenged them to fight, and they were obliged to dismiss the meeting. They went to a public house to take lodgings, and were followed by a mob. Being impressed that they were evil disposed, Elder Parry told the landlady, in the presence of the gang of ruffians, that he and his companion would take a walk before retiring for the night. He did not intend to return again, but said this to avoid being followed by the mob. After leaving the house he and his companion cast lots in the name of the Lord to know whether they should stay in that place for the night or go to another town near by. The lot fell for them to leave the place, and they did so. They arrived in the next town about midnight, and got lodgings at a public house, Elder Parry sleeping with a drunken fellow and his friend with a man that had fits several times during the night.

The next morning they returned for their valises, and met a man, who informed them that their enemies had been hunting for them during the night until seven o'clock in the morning. They had searched every part of the town, even among the tombstones, in the churchyard, and vowed that if they found the Elders they would kill them.

While preaching in a town in Wales, Elder Parry prophesied that before the end of that year (and it was then the month of September) there would be a branch of the Church of Jesus Christ raised up in that village. At that time there was but one member of the Church residing there; but before the year closed a branch with fourteen or fifteen members was organized.

Elder Parry relates some remarkable instances of healing by the power of God which he witnessed.

One was in the case of the sister who was afflicted with a cancer in her face, an account of which has already been given. He assisted Elder Abel Evans in administering to her, and testifies to her entire recovery.

Another case of miraculous healing was that of his brother-in-law, John Williams, who now resides in this Territory, and who was not a member of the Church at the time this occurred. He was also afflicted with a cancer which had completely taken away his lower lip and part of his chin and tongue. After trying in vain to get relief through the skill of physicians, he applied to the Elders of the Church to administer to him. They did so twice, and shortly after he received a new tongue, lip and chin.

Two children who were stricken with fever and ague and one with cancer, belonging to the same family, were also healed through the administration of the Elders.

Elder Parry testifies that many times while fulfilling his duties as an Elder of the Church of Jesus Christ he was attacked by mobs, who threw stones at him ; and although at times the stones flew past him in showers, he was never injured by them. Upon several occasions his enemies attempted to inflict upon him bodily injury, but they were frustrated in all their plans At one time they secured another man, thinking it to be Elder Parry, and maltreated him in a shameful manner.

Several of the most bitter enemies of the Church in those days died an unnatural death. One man, who was a sectarian minister, and one of the worst opposers to the work of God to be found in that vicinity, became ferocious like a mad dog, and had to be chained up for quite a while before his death.

Brother Parry was released from his labors as a traveling Elder in the Welsh conference, in the early part of the year 1856, and immediately prepared to emigrate to this country. Upon reaching Iowa City, on his journey westward, he was appointed captain of a company of one hundred persons. Provisions became scarce among the emigrants, and their rations were reduced to one-half pound of flour per day for each person. On account of this, some of the company on arriving at Council Bluffs concluded to remain there and work, and therefore left the camp. Upon learning this Brother Parry went back for them, and prevailed upon them to continue their journey. While trying to overtake the company, which was a considerable distance ahead, he was surrounded by a number of men who were very anxious that the emigrants who were with him should stay and work for them, and were angry at him for persuading them to leave. Some of the pursuing party were sent to procure tar and feathers to cover him with, while the others were guarding him. Their attention was attracted for a moment in another direction, when Elder Parry took advantage of the opportunity to escape by running towards the camp of the Saints. He was overtaken, however, before he reached it by two of the gang, who seized him by the collar, but he made some threats which frightened them and they let him go. After reaching camp he was still pursued by others who were mounted on horseback, and armed with revolvers, clubs, etc., but he escaped their recognition by changing his clothing. The mobocrats finally returned to Council Bluffs without having accomplished their object, for Elder Parry's influence over the discouraged men prevailed, and they decided to continue their journey.

CHAPTER IV.

JOHN T. EVANS' STATEMENT—A SICK AND HELPLESS WOMAN HEALED ON BEING BAPTIZED—RELAPSE AND DEATH AFTER APOSTASY—SAINTS REQUIRED TO RENOUNCE THER RELIGION OR LOSE THEIR SITUATIONS—CHOLERA EPIDEMIC— HEALED ACCORDING TO FAITH—PRIVATE DISCUSSION WITH A MALIGNANT WHO TAKES THE CHOLERA AND BEGS THE ELDERS TO CURE HIM—HEALED AND THEN BAPTIZED—CURIOUS MANNER IN WHICH FOOD AND LODGING WERE PROVIDED.

ELDER JOHN T. EVANS, now of Salt Lake City, spent about eight years when a young man in preaching the gospel in his native country—Wales. During about five years of this time he labored as a traveling Elder in North Wales, one of the very hardest of missionary fields, where he traveled and preached without purse or scrip. Much of the time he labored alone, for, although many different Elders were sent at various times by the president of the mission to assist him, they generally became discouraged on account of the persecution and hardships they were forced to endure and soon abandoned their labors.

The interesting incidents connected with his labors in that land which Elder Evans can relate would fill a volume.

Upon one occasion he and four other Elders were sent to an iron manufacturing district about seven miles from Neath to introduce the gospel. Among their first converts were a man by the name of William Howells and his family. This man on embracing the gospel received a strong testimony of its divinity and was fearless in declaring it unto others. He had a sister who had been so sick and helpless as to be bed-ridden for three-and-a-half years. She was a member of the Baptist church, but on hearing the doctrines of the Latter-day Saints explained she soon became dissatisfied with her religion; and when her brother testified to her that the gospel had been restored to the earth through the Prophet Joseph Smith, with all its former gifts and blessings, she declared her intention to be baptized. Her husband was bitterly opposed to the gospel, but all the reason, ridicule and persuasion that he could use failed to turn her from her purpose. She was resolute, and so zealous withal that she made a special request to be baptized on Sunday, between eleven and twelve o'clock, that the people of the whole neighborhood might see the ceremony, and had word circulated to that effect. It was a novel thing in that region to see Latter-day Saints baptizing, and the result was, that about three thousand persons assembled on the bank of the stream to witness it. She was carried from the house to the stream, the distance of about half a mile in a chair, and there Elder Evans, assisted by a man named David Matthews, carried her into the water and baptized her.

She was rewarded for her faith by being entirely restored to health, and that too, instantaneously, for she walked out of the water and to her home.

This public manifestation of the power of God seemed to be the signal for commencing a perfect storm of opposition against the Saints. Through the influence of sectarian ministers with the proprietors of the iron works a great pressure was brought to bear against the Saints. It was claimed that they were Chartists, that is, members of a political organization which had caused a great deal of trouble throughout the kingdom a short time previously, and other lies equally unreasonable were circulated about them to make them odious and unpopular.

The five Elders who had been doing the preaching and baptizing, and who were dependent upon their labor in the iron works for their living, were informed by their employers that they must renounce the "heresy" which they taught as religion, or lose their positions. They chose the latter.

About two hundred of their converts were also employed in the iron works. They were given one month's time to renounce their religion or likewise lose their situations. All efforts to obtain employment elsewhere without a recommendation from their last employers proved unavailing, on account of the rumors against their characters, and finally, when they were brought to the test, about half of them chose to renounce their religion rather than lose their work. The others were discharged and scattered to different parts in search of employment. Many of them suffered severely for want of the necessaries of life, and were only kept from starving by the collections taken up for their benefit among the more fortunate Saints in other parts of the mission.

Among others who yielded to the pressure which the enemies of the Saints brought to bear against them, was the sister who had been healed on being baptized. Notwithstanding her former zeal and resolution, and the miraculous power of God which she had experienced, she abandoned the faith. She perhaps thought she had no further need of God's mercy, but if so, the sequel proved how sadly she was mistaken, for she was soon prostrated as before and lingered in that condition until she died.

In the summer of 1849 the cholera prevailed throughout Wales to an alarming extent. The mortality was so great in some places that a perfect panic ensued. The Elders, however, continued their labors, undaunted by the disease, administering to the sick day and night, and the faith of the Saints was so great that they almost invariably recovered. A local Elder by the name of Thomas Jones, who was a man of some property, and not obliged to work for his living, spent his whole time while the disease prevailed in visiting among the sick. He carried a bottle of consecrated oil about in his pocket to anoint them with, and administered to all whom he found afflicted, and out of the whole number only one died, and he was the only one who had taken the medicine prescribed by a doctor. The town regulations required the sick to have a doctor, but as a rule his medicine was thrown into the fire instead of being taken by the patients who belonged to the Church.

One of the preachers who had violently opposed the Saints became alarmed at the spread of the epidemic and attempted to flee and escape from it, but it overtook him, and after three days of terrible agony he died.

Another preacher by the name of Jenkins, who had been an enemy to the Saints, was stricken with the cholera and sent for Elder Evans to administer to him. That he should do so will be considered all the more remarkable when the history of their early acquaintance is known:

Elder Evans, while laboring in Pembrokeshire, obtained the use of the town hall, in a place called Fishguard, to hold meeting in and lighted it at his own expense. When the meeting had fairly commenced and he was in the act of preaching to a rather large audience, the whole of the lights in the room were extinguished simultaneously, according to a preconcerted plan, and a rush was made by the rabble towards the end of the room where the Elder stood. A tall man, who happened to be standing near Elder Evans, immediately placed his hand on the latter's shoulder, and said, "Young man, come out of here, or you will be hurt!" and leading the way, proceeded with him around one side of the room and out through the door, leaving the crowd rushing and jamming and shrieking to get at the Elder, whom they still supposed to be at the farther end of the hall.

The stranger took Elder Evans to a public house, saying that he would like to have a talk with him, and on arriving there sent for Mr. Jenkins, the Baptist preacher of the place, who had been at the meeting, and probably engaged in urging the rabble on, to come there and have a private discussion. He came, and his principal argument consisted of abuse and the rehearsal of all the absurd stories which he had ever heard about the Saints. Although an educated man he seemed unable to cope with Elder Evans in the discussion of religion from a Bible standpoint.

The friend who had delivered Brother Evans from the mob finally interrupted them by exclaiming, "Mr. Jenkins, you are no match for this young man in discussing from the Bible; you had better go to college again!"

Mr. Jenkins seemed considerably chagrined at this, and gave it up.

The next time Elder Evans met this preacher it was some months later, and, probably remembering the discussion, Mr.

A GIRL AFFLICTED WITH THE CHOLERA HEALED. 53

Jenkins then treated him with some degree of respect. It was that very night that he was stricken with the cholera, and knowing that Elder Evans was in the village he sent his brother to beg of him to come and cure him. Brother Evans, and a man named John Nicholas who was staying with him, got out of bed and went to the sick man, and found him, doubled up with the cholera and in great agony. The Elder informed him, in answer to his appeal for relief, that the blessings of the gospel were not for men of his class, who were determined to oppose the work of God, but for the Saints. He said, "I will administer to you on one condition only, and that is that you repent of your sins and covenant with the Lord to forsake them and embrace the gospel if He spares your life."

"But," said the preacher, writhing with pain, "I have an appointment out to preach for my own church."

"You must forego that," said Elder Evans, "and preach such doctrines no more, or I will not administer to you."

The sick man agreed, and the brethren placed their hands upon his head, rebuked the disease and prayed for his recovery, and he was immediately healed. The next day he was baptized, and afterwards became an efficient preacher of the true gospel, endured much persecution for his religion in that country, emigrated to Utah with a handcart company and finally apostatized when Johnson's army came here.

Brother Evans and a man named Thomas Harris were upon one occasion called on to administer to a young girl who was so convulsed with the cholera that she did not look like a human being, and so near dead that she was black. A number of Saints were present at the time, whose faith was centered on her recovery, and several unbelievers were also there. The Elders administered to her, and while their hands were upon her head all signs of the disease vanished, and she was immediately restored to health.

A rather curious circumstance occurred while Elder Evans was laboring in North Wales in company with Peter Davis. They were traveling as usual without purse or scrip, and had been two days without food, when they entered a village and applied at a store kept by a man named Jones to try to sell a few tracts with which to procure some food.

On learning what kind of tracts they were, the store-keeper refused to purchase, and they tramped on. The next place they entered was a shoe-maker's shop, where they asked the privilege of warming themselves by the fire, for they were almost frozen, it being extremely cold weather and the month of February. Some of the shoe-makers became interested in their conversation and one of them proffered to try and find a place for them to stay over night. He returned, however, after a while, to say that the Methodist preacher of that circuit was to occupy the spare bed which he expected to procure for them. He, therefore, recommended them to proceed some distance farther till they came to a farm house, to which he directed them, where he had no doubt they could get lodgings and food.

The Elders trudged along, but when they arrived at the farm house it was evident that the family had retired for the night, for there was no light to be seen. They noticed a barn, however, standing convenient to the roadside, which seemed to offer shelter for them at least, and they entered it and burrowed into a heap of straw they found there. They lay in that position for some time, shivering with the cold and trying in vain to go to sleep, when suddenly they heard some one outside call out, "Hello! you men; come out here!" Their first thought was that some one had detected them while in the act of seeking shelter in the barn and informed the police, who were about to arrest them as vagrants. They, therefore, remained as quiet as possible until the call had been repeated several times, when they concluded they might as well answer, whatever might be the consequences. As soon as they inquired what was wanted, the person informed them that he would find a place for them to stay if they would come out. Thinking some treachery might be meant, they declined with thanks, and told him they could get along where they were. He, however, urged them to go with him, saying he would take them to a place where they could have a good supper and a comfortable bed to sleep in. They accordingly came out and accompanied the stranger, whom they had never seen before,

PROVIDED FOR IN A CURIOUS MANNER.   55

back to the village and to the very store where they had tried to sell the tracts There they found a warm welcome, a good supper and a comfortable bed. But now for the sequel:

A young girl who happened to be in the shoe-shop where they called and who overheard the conversation, afterwards had occasion to call at Jones' store, and repeated it to the proprietor's daughter. The sympathy of the girls was aroused at the thoughts of the two young and strange preachers seeking lodgings and food that cold night, and when Miss Jones retired to bed she found it impossible to go to sleep. Her teeth rattled and she shook and chilled all over although she was in a comfortable bed and in a warm house. Nor could the family prevent her from chilling although they did all they could to warm her. In the midst of her shivering she kept bewailing the fate of the two young preachers, whom she felt sure would suffer that cold night, and finally she prevailed upon her brother to go in search of them and bring them back to their house, that they might have some supper and a comfortable bed to sleep in.

As soon as her brother had started on his errand of mercy the girl ceased to chill and, in fact, got up, dressed herself and helped at preparing supper for the brethren before they arrived. It was not until the next morning that they learned the secret of the kindness shown them and saw in what a curious manner the Lord had operated in preserving them from possible death by freezing and providing them with the food which they needed so badly.

It was quite a common thing in early days in the Welsh mission for the power of the devil to be manifested in what were called the Saints' meetings—that is, testimony or sacramental meetings. The evil one seemed to be always on the alert to operate through some one, and the power of the Priesthood invariably had to be exerted to banish the evil influences from the meeting. Although not apparent at the time, experience generally proved that the persons through whom the evil one operated were not serving God as they should do—they were either doubting the divinity of the principles which they had embraced or they had broken the sacred covenants which they had made with the Almighty and gone into transgression. Very frequently, after being relieved of the evil spirits which possessed them such persons would, in a spirit of penitence and humility, acknowledge their faults and ask forgiveness, but occasionally persons would be found who were not willing to do this, but continued in sin and were a source of trouble and disturbance to the Saints whenever they happened to be present at their meetings; and it sometimes occurred that the spirits which possessed them were so stubborn and determined not to yield that the brethren really found it difficult to cope with them.

In the latter part of the year 1848, the Elders laboring in the Merthyr Tydvil branch had a great deal of trouble with two young women of that branch who very frequently were possessed of evil spirits. They were such a source of annoyance in the meetings that, on the day of a general conference which was to be held about the close of the year, they were cautioned, by Elder Dan Jones who then presided there, against attending the meeting. To this, however, they paid no attention, and when the meeting was opened, it was only too apparent that they were there. In a short time the meeting was in such an uproar, through the raving and shrieking of those girls, that the speaker could not be heard. Some of the Elders were immediately sent to cast the evil spirits out of them, but they failed to do so, and with difficulty the girls were carried into an adjoining room.

When a presiding Elder has the spirit of his office upon him it is his privilege to know the proper course to take in any emergency. It is his privilege to enjoy communion with the Holy Spirit and have the Lord dictate through him that which will be for the best good of the members over whom he is set to preside. It is also his privilege to discern by what spirit the people with whom he is brought in contact are actuated.

It would seem that Elder Dan Jones had the spirit of discernment on that occasion and was inspired to take the wisest course in dealing with the girls and the stubborn spirits by which they were possessed. He was satisfied that they were wilfully sinful, or the spirit of God would not be withdrawn from them and the devil suffered to exercise such power over them. He therefore proposed that they be cut off from the

Church on account of their transgressions, and the Saints assembled voted unanimously to that effect. No sooner had they done so than the evil spirits left the girls and they became rational. When they were no longer members of the Church, the devil had no further need to try to annoy the Saints through them. The result was that the girls afterwards saw what their sin had brought them to, repented of it and made public acknowledgement before the Saints, after which they were re-baptized and were no more troubled by evil spirits.

CHAPTER V.

JUDGMENT UPON OPPOSERS—TWO MEN KILLED BY THEIR HORSES—HORRIBLE DEATH OF ANOTHER—EIGHT PREACHERS GO DOWN AFTER OPPOSING ELDER EVANS—A MAN SAVED FROM BLEEDING TO DEATH BY THE PRAYER OF FAITH—A SISTER HEALED—WOMAN CURED OF A BLOODY ISSUE ON BEING BAPTIZED—ESCAPE THE FURY OF A MOB BY THE SPIRIT'S WARNING—A WARNING THROUGH THE GIFT OF TONGUES.

IN numbers of instances in Brother John T. Evans' experience he had evidence of the judgments of the Almighty being visited upon those who opposed him.

On one occasion he and another Elder visited a village in Montgomeryshire, North Wales, to try to effect an opening. They failed to obtain a house to hold meeting in, but nevertheless they announced to the inhabitants that they would be back there one week from that time to preach to them. There seemed to be a strong spirit of opposition to them there, and on their again visiting the place and attempting to preach in the street opposite a public house, two men emerged from the rear of the tavern leading a couple of fractious and high-spirited horses. They immediately commenced manœuvering the animals in the midst of the crowd who had gathered to listen to the preaching. It was evidently a preconcerted plan to break up the meeting, and it succeeded, for the people scattered and the Elders were forced to retire, and as they did so they were followed by a crowd of roughs who pelted them with stones till they had got clear of the village. Within two weeks from that time one of the men who had helped to break up the meeting by leading his horse into the crowd was kicked by the same animal and died from the effects of it, and the other man was thrown from his horse and killed. The people of that region regarded the summary death of these two men as a judgment sent upon them for opposing the Elders, and they therefore treated them with more respect afterwards.

Another case occurred in Elder Evans' native place, where he was sent by Captain Dan Jones to introduce the gospel. An old shoemaker who had known and been friendly to him from his childhood, on hearing him preach came out and denounced the doctrine he taught as heretical and "Mormonism" as a delusion. He was so bitter that he even followed Brother Evans from place to place and railed against him almost like a madman. He had not pursued this course very long when he was stricken down with a peculiar kind of sickness which none of the doctors who saw him understood anything about, although numbers of them visited him. One of his arms was paralyzed and he had such a raging fever that he felt as if it was consuming him. He begged of his friends to throw cold water on him to keep him from burning up, and the doctors, not knowing what else to do for his relief, advised that it be done. Accordingly those who were waiting upon him continued dashing cold water upon him while he remained alive, and he died raving and cursing "Mormonism" and every person connected with it.

While preaching in that same region Elder Evans was sent for by a very wealthy and influential man named Nathaniel Rowlands, who wished him to come and preach at his house. He had once heard Elder Abel Evans, preach and became somewhat interested in the doctrines he taught, and wanted to learn more of them. After preaching at his house he went to a village about a mile distant to fill an appointment. At this village a literary gathering or *eisteddfod* was being held, composed of the best educated men of the region, who were in the habit of meeting to compare their literary and musical compositions and compete for prizes. This association comprized quite a number of ministers of various denominations, and they, knowing that Elder Evans was going to preach in the village on the same evening upon which they were to hold their meeting, decided to go and oppose him publicly and expose his doctrines to the ridicule of his congregation. They, therefore, sent one of their number to Elder Evans' meeting to detain him until their meeting was over.

This man came, and at the close of Elder Evans' sermon he began asking him questions, and thus detained him until a late hour, and the congregation, knowing the character of the inquisitor, stayed to see the end of the controversy. Finally, eight other preachers from the *eisteddfod* came and announced to the Elder their intention. Elder Evans was greatly surprised to see such an array of talent unitedly opposed to him, but he did not feel to shrink from the contest, for he knew he had the truth on his side. In the outset some of the more independent persons in the audience stated that if the fallacy of the young man's doctrines was to be exposed, he should first be allowed to state briefly what his doctrines were. The preachers assented to this and Elder Evans explained, one after another, the first principles of the gospel, in as plain a manner as possible, and they in turn sought to controvert and ridicule them. When he got to the subject of baptism a division occurred among the preachers, some of them being Baptists and others holding baptism as non-essential. They soon got to denouncing each other as vehemently as they had the young Elder just before, and when they almost got to blows the audience interfered and the meeting was broken up, leaving a far more favorable feeling towards Elder Evans than had before existed.

When the news of this reached Mr. Rowlands he was very indignant, and he immediately wrote to each of the preachers, denouncing his action in interfering with the young Elder, whom he had known from childhood as honest and conscientious, and every way deserving of respect. The result was, the preachers lost caste from that very time and sunk into oblivion, despised by all who knew them.

While Elder Evans was laboring in Pembrokeshire a man by the name of Thomas Evans broke a blood vessel and bled inwardly, the blood also issuing from his nose and mouth profusely. Doctors were called in and tried in vain to stop the hemorrhage. Brother Evans and another Elder on learning of the man's condition went to see him. He had then grown so weak that he was scarcely able to speak, but he made known that he desired them to administer to him. They complied with his request, and on taking their hands from his head it was noticed that the bleeding had stopped, and the man recovered from that time, although it was some time before he regained his strength, as he had lost so much blood.

Near the same time and in the same region a sister in the Church, named Morgan, was taken very sick. Her friends did all they could for her, but she continued growing worse. When she had grown so bad that the persons waiting upon her expected her to die almost hourly, she fell asleep and dreamed that Elder Evans came and laid his hands upon her and she recovered immediately. On relating the dream to her friends, they tried to find out where Brother Evans was, and sent to different parts of the country in search of him, without finding him, however; but during the day Elder Evans happened to call at the house where the sick woman was. She saw him as he passed the window before he entered the door and she declared afterwards that the sight of him caused her pain to vanish, and when he laid his hands upon her head she was healed instantly, and arose and ate her supper.

One of the most remarkable cases of healing that ever occurred in Brother Evans' experience was that of a woman who had been afflicted with a bloody issue for thirty years, and who had been given up by the doctors as incurable. On hearing the gospel she believed, and requested baptism. Notwithstanding the protests of her friends, who all declared that if she went into the water it would kill her, she determined to do so, and Elder Evans baptized her. From that very time she was cured of her affliction and was no more troubled by it.

ESCAPES THE FURY OF THE MOB. 61

In illustration of the providential way in which the Elders are sometimes preserved when their enemies seek to destroy them, Brother Evans relates the following: In a village in Pembrokeshire in which he had often preached, a man by the name of Thomas, who had listened to his testimony and was a believer but had not made up his mind to be baptized, was taken sick with the cholera. When the disease had got such a hold upon him that he felt that he must die, he became very anxious to be baptized, and sent for his brother, who was an Elder in the Church, and demanded baptism at his hands. He expressed no hopes of living, he fully expected to die, and to gratify him his brother baptized him. The man died soon afterwards as he had expected to, but at the coroner's inquest which was held over the body, on the fact being known that he was baptized, a great uproar was raised. His brother was arrested, charged with murder, and the Elders who had labored in that region were threatened with the vengeance of the populace if they ever returned. John Thomas was in time tried for his brother's murder, and acquitted, the evidence being clear that he died from cholera and not from being baptized. Soon afterwards Elder John Morris, who was president of the Pembrokeshire conference, and Brother Evans, who was his counselor, called at the village and put up as usual at the house of an old gentleman named Noat, who was a member of the Church. Before retiring for the night they felt impressed to leave that house, and go to another and stay. It was fortunate that they did so, for, if they had failed to act upon the warning of the Spirit, they would probably have forfeited their lives as a consequence. In the night a mob broke open the doors of Noat's house and searched for the Elders, whom they supposed to be there. Failing to find them, they dragged old Brother Noat from his house and abused him most shamefully, because he would not inform them where the Elders were. The Elders, on hearing of the outrage the next morning, went to the house; but were seen by some of the mob, and had to flee for their lives, being stoned out of the place.

As an example of the manner in which the gifts of tongues and the interpretation of the same were enjoyed by the Saints in the Welsh mission in an early day, Brother Evans relates the following: It was customary at that time for the Saints in emigrating from Wales to sail from Swansea to Liverpool. A couple or three days after a company had started in this way, many of them having gone from Aberdare, a "Saints' meeting" was being held in the latter place, when a young man was led to speak in tongues. On the interpretation being given by another person present, it was stated that the company of Saints who had sailed for Liverpool were in danger of being wrecked, and were praying very earnestly for their deliverance, and wishing that their friends at home would also pray for them. The man who presided over the meeting supposed from the length of time which had elapsed after the company had sailed that they must have reached Liverpool before that time. He therefore preferred to act upon his own judgment to accepting the Spirit's warning, and dismissed the meeting without offering a prayer for the safety of their friends. A few days afterwards news reached Aberdare that the company had been all but lost on the voyage, and at the time that their friends were holding their meeting they were in the greatest peril.

CHAPTER VI.

THOMAS D. GILES' EXPERIENCE—HIS HEAD CRUSHED AND SPLIT OPEN BY A TON OF COAL FALLING UPON IT—HEALED BY THE POWER OF GOD—A DEAF AND DUMB MAN RECEIVES HIS HEARING AND SPEECH ON BEING BAPTIZED, ETC.

BROTHER THOMAS D. GILES, of Salt Lake City, was connected with the Church and labored considerably in the ministry in Wales soon after the introduction of the gospel in that land. He relates many curious circumstances connected with his conversion to the gospel and his early experience in the same, some of which we will give to our readers substantially as he tells them:

ELDER THOS. D. GILES' EXPERIENCE.

Brother Giles was a Baptist when he was a young man, and an earnest seeker after truth wherever it was to be found. The first time he met his friend Abel Evans after that gentleman had joined the Church, he was asked by him what he thought of the Latter-day Saints. Brother Giles replied that he knew nothing about them. Brother Evans then predicted that he soon would know something about them, and, more than that, he and his father's family would soon be baptized by them. Brother Giles thought but little of this prediction at the time, but it was soon literally fulfilled, for on hearing the gospel preached he was convinced of its truth, and on the 1st of November, 1844, he was baptized by Elder Abel Evans. He bears his solemn testimony now that as soon as the Elders placed their hands upon his head and confirmed him a member of the Church the power of the Holy Ghost filled his system, brought joy to his heart and gave him an assurance that his sins were forgiven, for which he had been praying for many years. His father was also prepared to receive the gospel as soon as he heard it preached, for he had for a long time been inquiring after a church organized after the pattern given by our Savior and His apostles, and possessing the various gifts which were formerly enjoyed by the Saints. The result was that he and the whole of his family were soon baptized.

About seventeen months after he was baptized Elder Giles was called to labor as a missionary in Monmouthshire, where he soon baptized a goodly number of people, organized about thirty branches of the Church and had the satisfaction of seeing his converts enjoy the gifts of the gospel, such as speaking in tongues, interpreting the same, healing the sick, casting out evil spirits, etc. He had much opposition to meet, and suffered considerable persecution, but was upheld by the power of God, and had great joy in his labors. When holding outdoor meetings he was frequently interrupted by persons who were influenced by the sectarian ministers of the region. One man in particular, named Daniels, was very persistent in opposing him and trying to break up his meetings, and on one occasion after doing so he declared that if the Elders attempted to hold meeting again at the same place the following Sunday he would have men enough there to mob them out of the place. Before the next Sunday came, however, the man was in his grave, having been accidentally killed while at his work.

The first person baptized under Brother Giles' administration was a man named Wm. Lewis, who immediately opened his house for the Elders to hold meetings in. But the Saints soon numbered so many that his house would not contain them. The Elders then applied to a tavern keeper for a large room in which to hold their meetings, which he very kindly granted them, and in a short time he and all his family were converted and baptized, and gave up their tavern. Baptisms occurred every night in the week, and in a short time that branch numbered two hundred and three. In time a still larger hall was required in which to convene, and the Elders applied to a Mr. Davis, who owned a large building called "The Greyhound Hall," to obtain the use of it. He, however, could not think of allowing the "Mormons" to meet in his hall, as he feared it would injure his business and destroy his influence. But he soon had reason to regret taking such an illiberal course, as he met with a series of losses through having his animals suddenly sicken and die, and could only attribute his bad luck to the displeasure of the Almighty at his refusal to grant the Saints the use of his hall. After that he was glad to have them use it. Among others baptized was the leader of the Baptist choir as well as most of his principal singers, and as a consequence the singing in the meetings of the Saints became quite an attractive feature.

The faith in the ordinances of the gospel displayed by the Saints among whom Brother Giles labored was quite remarkable. The feeling with most of them on being taken sick was that if they could only have the Elders come and lay their hands upon them they would be well, and the result was generally according to their faith. Brother Wm. Lewis, of whom mention has already been made, was taken seriously sick on one occasion and was unable to leave his bed. His first thought was to send for Elder Giles to come and administer to him. He visited him as requested, and, on entering the door, called out cheerily, asking him what he meant by lying in bed, and told him to get up and come down stairs. So great was the sick man's faith that he sprang out of bed on hearing the voice and obeyed, and when Brother Giles had administered to him he was as well as he ever had been.

Similar faith was manifested by the Saints when the cholera prevailed in that land, and Brother Giles testifies that every one so afflicted whom he or the other Elders laboring with him administered to, recovered. This was certainly remarkable, considering the very great number of unbelievers who died there of that dread malady. One case in particular Brother Giles mentions, that of a sister named Dudley, who was so bad that she had turned black and whose sunken eyes indicated that she had not many minutes to live. None of the friends who surrounded her had any hopes of her living except her husband. He called for Elder Giles to administer to her and when he did so she was restored to health and is now living in Utah.

About the same time a Mrs. Davies, who was not in the Church, sent for Elders Giles and Dudley to administer to her, as she was very sick and confined to her bed. They did so, and her faith made her whole. After that she and her husband joined the Church, and are in Utah now, true Latter-day Saints.

On another occasion, when Elder Giles was on a visit to his father's house, he was sent for to administer to a neighbor lady, who had been sick and confined to her bed for a considerable length of time. When he went to see her she was suffering the most excruciating pain, but when he had anointed her and rebuked her disease all pain vanished and she was restored to health. She afterwards came to Utah and frequently testified of the miraculous manner in wich she was healed.

Brother Giles himself met with a terrible accident, and the power of God manifested in preserving his life and restoring him to health, was not less remarkable than in the cases before mentioned. On the 23rd of July, 1843, he visited the Llanelly branch of the Church, where he held meeting out of doors in the forenoon and in the afternoon attended a sacrament meeting. At the latter meeting permission was given for any of the Saints to speak as they might feel led by the Spirit. Among others Elder Giles was moved upon to speak in tongues, and the interpretation of what he said was given to the president of the branch, Elder John Morgan, as follows: "My servant, watch, for thy life is in danger; but through thy faith thy life shall be spared!"

Feeling sure that there was something prophetic about this, Elder Giles warned Brother Morgan at the close of the meeting to be careful, and not to be out late at night, lest some plot might be laid by his enemies to take his life. He also said that he would try to take care of himself, and avoid danger, lest it might be himself that the warning was intended for.

On the following Wednesday, the 26th of July, Brother Giles went to his work as usual in the coal mine, and in a short time after he had commenced work a large piece of coal, weighing about two thousand pounds fell upon him. He was in a stooping posture at the time, being about to pick up a piece of coal that lay in front of him, and when he was knocked down his head lodged between this and the mass of coal that fell upon him. His head was split open from the back of the crown down to his eyes. One of his eyes was also completely cut out of the socket, and the other crushed so that it ran out.

He was taken home, and two physicians came and examined his head. They declined doing anything for him, as they said it was not possible for him to live over two hours. However, after a great deal of persuasion, they consented to wash off his head, pick the pieces of coal out of it and sew up the wounds. They also left medicine for him to take, such as they thought suitable for the case, but he refused to take a drop of it. He remembered the promise of the Lord, that through faith his life should be spared, and felt to hold on to it and claim a blessing at the hands of the Almighty. The Saints of the branch in which he lived were very faithful and kind, and did all they possibly could under the circumstances for his comfort.

On the third day after the accident Elder William S. Phillips, the president of the Welsh mission, anointed him with consecrated oil, laid his hands upon his head and blessed him in the name of Jesus Christ. Brother Giles testifies that the healing power of the Holy Spirit did rest upon him at that time, for he got out of bed and walked across two rooms, back and forth. On the ninth day after the accident he sang a song for some of his friends who had called to see him, and in four weeks he traveled twelve miles in company with two of the brethren to visit his father and mother and the president of the branch. On the fourth Sunday after the accident, being called upon, he spoke in a public meeting in the afternoon and evening.

Soon after that he was called upon to travel throughout the mission and bear his testimony and preach to the people, in company with Elder John Jones, and he did so.

While thus engaged he visited Newport, and learned the particulars of a miracle that had occurred there a short time previous. A young man named Reuben Brinkworth, who had been deaf and dumb for a number of years, manifested a desire to be baptized, and on receiving that ordinance at the hands of Elder Nash, in whose house he resided, both his hearing and speech were immediately restored to him.

Brother Giles visited this young man and questioned him in regard to the miracle, and was assured by him that when he went into the water to be baptized he could neither hear nor speak, but as soon as he was baptized he could do both. Brother Nash also bore his testimony to the same facts.

Near the same time that Brother Giles met with his accident a friend of his, named David Davis, who was living in Merthyr, was almost crushed to a pulp by the roof of a coal mine falling upon him. When he was dug out Elder William Phillips and some other brethren laid their hands upon him and promised him that he should live and be healed. While their hands were upon his head, his broken ribs and other bones were heard coming together with a noise which was quite perceptible. Brother Davis, who was a truthful, honest man, lived to travel about Wales and testify of this miracle and follow his daily labor as if no such accident had ever occurred. He afterwards emigrated to the United States, and is perhaps yet alive.

CHAPTER VII.

SCENE IN THE EXPERIENCE OF WM. J. SMITH—A STRANGE PROPHECY AND ITS WONDERFUL FULFILLMENT.

IN February, 1856, Elder William J. Smith, who was on a mission in England, was appointed by the Presidency of the Church in that land to preside over the Warwickshire conference. Under his ministrations many were baptized into the Church in Coventry, which stirred up the clergy of that city against him to such an extent that they specially enjoined it upon their scripture readers to warn the people against going to hear the "Mormons."

Elder Smith determined to deliver a series of eight lectures on the first principles of the gospel, at Spurn End chapel, the regular meeting place of the Saints; and to secure attendance he placarded Coventry with large bills announcing his intention. This caused many to come and hear him.

On the Sunday morning announced for the sixth lecture Elder Smith was so sick that he was unable to arise from his bed. In this extremity he prayed earnestly to the Lord to heal him, so that he could fill his appointment. It was with much difficulty that he went to the morning's meeting, but being resolved to do his utmost, he addressed the Saints, and, the Spirit of God resting upon him, he was much strengthened and was enabled to fill his appointment in the afternoon.

The meeting was a very crowded one; all classes apparently were represented; scripture readers were present to take notes, while numbers, probably hundreds, were unable to obtain admission.

In the rear of the chapel ran the line of railway that connected Coventry with Nuneaton, and in that portion of its road it was built upon arches high above the ground. These were so near the chapel that whenever a train passed, it not only made a great noise, but perceptibly shook the building.

A STRANGE PROPHECY FULFILLED. 69

Elder Smith's audience, though so large, was a very attentive one, but shortly after he had commenced speaking a train came thundering by, causing the minds of the people to be distracted from his teachings. Feeling annoyed at the interruption, the speaker suddenly stopped talking, paused for a few moments and then exclaimed, "Babylon! confusion! I cannot speak an hour without being interrupted by the railway," and then, stretching out his hand, he continued, "In the name of Jesus Christ, my Master, that railway arch shall fall to the ground." Elder Smith then continued his sermon. When he had done, he had mingled feelings; he could scarcely understand why he was prompted to utter such a prophecy; he felt that if he had left that out it would have been the best discourse he ever preached. But the words were uttered and could not be recalled; they had been heard by scores, many of whom were not friends of the Saints; still he felt impressed that what he had prophesied was by the Spirit of God, and that gave him peace.

His words were reported to nine clergymen, who made it their business to have competent judges examine the arches and discover if possible if there was any cause for a statement and prophecy such as his. These gentlemen declared the arches to be sound, that there were no better in England, and consequently Brother Smith was ridiculed and derided as a false prophet.

Shortly afterwards Elder Smith was called away from Coventry by the presidency of the mission, and appointed to succeed Elder Henry Lunt in the presidency of the Newcastle-on-Tyne pastorate. He left Warwickshire without seeing his prophecy fulfilled; but within a few weeks a heavy rain fell and undermined the arches, and nineteen out of twenty-one fell to the ground, leaving only two standing. Through this fall much damage was done to the contiguous residences and other property.

Brother Henry Russell, who now lives at Union, in Salt Lake County, was at that time a lamp-lighter in Coventry. He was engaged in lighting the street lamps when this destruction took place. He was just about to pass under one of the arches when it fell, and he probably would have been killed had he not been stopped by a policeman and detained until the danger was over.

Thus is the saying of the Lord corroborated, that what His servants declare by His Spirit He will fulfill.

REMARKABLE HEALINGS.

MARTIN H. PECK'S TESTIMONY OF A NUMBER OF REMARKABLE CASES OF HEALING—A BROKEN ARM, A CRUSHED LEG, ETC., HEALED IMMEDIATELY.

BROTHER MARTIN H. PECK, of Salt Lake City, relates a series of cases of healing that occurred in his family and under his administration. He joined the Church in Vermont, in 1833, and about two years later, while on a visit to a place about nine miles from where he lived, he received word from his wife at home that their child was lying at the point of death and she desired him to come home immediately and bring an Elder with him. He was not more surprised at learning of his son's dangerous condition than of the faith in the ordinances of the gospel which his wife manifested, by wanting an Elder to lay hands on the child; for she had not then joined the Church or manifested much interest in the gospel. He was therefore almost as much pleased on his wife's account as he was pained on account of his child on receiving the news. Taking Elder James Snow with him, he hastened home, and found the little fellow lying helpless and in a very low condition in his mother's arms. Brother Peck only held the office of a Priest at the time, so Elder Snow administered to the child alone, and while doing so the little fellow dozed off into a quiet slumber, and when he awoke he was as well as he ever had been.

Soon afterwards Brother Peck himself was taken extremely ill, and to all appearances seemed about to die. He even lost his sight and was in the greatest agony, but Elder John Badger was called in and rebuked the disease and blessed him, and he was healed immediately. On describing his symptoms afterwards to a friend who was an experienced physician, he was assured that his was an extreme case, and it was doubtful if medical skill could have saved him.

Near the same time his son Joseph was troubled with a couple of swellings on the glands of his neck which threatened to choke him. After various remedies had been tried without avail a physician was consulted, who declared the boy could not live long if they continued to grow, and recommended that a surgical operation be performed to remove them, although even that, he admitted, would be very dangerous. Brother Peck concluded not to act upon his advice, and he sent for some Elders instead and had them anoint and lay hands upon him The result was that in a few days the swellings had entirely disappeared.

From Vermont Brother Peck removed to Ohio, and while there a great deal of sickness prevailed and many deaths occurred in his neighborhood. The doctors seemed to be entirely baffled in their efforts to cope with the disease. Among others stricken down was Brother Peck's son, William. He lay unconscious all day with his eyes turned back in his head, and apparently in a dying condition. A number of neighbors called in to see him and urged Brother Peck to send for a doctor. He told them, however, that he could not have much confidence in doctors' skill after seeing the children which they attended die off, as they had done, like rotten sheep. He preferred to have nothing to do with them. Nor did he feel like administering to the boy while unbelievers were in the house. His wife happened to be away from home, and he felt confident that when she returned their united faith would result in obtaining a blessing from the Almighty. Some of the neighbors in their solicitude stayed with the boy all day, and doubtless thought Brother Peck an unfeeling wretch, as he would not send for a doctor. On the return of Sister Peck she, too, refused to have a physician, and so the neighbors left in disgust. As soon as they had done so the parents called mightily upon the Lord to spare their child's life and Brother Peck rebuked the disease, and he was healed instantly.

72   EARLY SCENES IN CHURCH HISTORY.

But a few days had elapsed when their son James was taken suddenly very sick, and a neighbor hastened to Brother Peck's shop to inform him if something were not done immediately for his relief he would be dead. He also offered his services to wait upon him. Brother Peck thanked him for his kindness but declined accepting the offer. On reaching his home and seeing the condition of the child, which was truly alarming, he and his wife referred the case to the Lord, with the same result as in the previous case.

A rather curious case was that of a young lady who lived in Brother Peck's family who was afflicted with a most distressing cough, from which she could get no relief. It seemed as if she would almost choke with it. On being administered to by the Elders she was relieved immediately, and never coughed again for two weeks, when, on getting in a passion, the cough returned.

There was a doctor by the name of Harvey Tate living neighbor to Brother Peck in Ohio, who became somewhat interested in the doctrines of the Latter-day Saints, and for the purpose of learning more concerning them made a visit to his house. While he was there Brother Peck's son James was brought home with a broken arm, caused by his falling from a tree. The fracture was about three inches above the wrist joint, and so complete that his arm formed a right angle at the place where it was broken. The doctor set and bandaged it, and the boy was put in bed. The pain was so great, however, that he could scarcely endure it, and after the doctor had gone he begged his father to "bless" him, saying he knew that would cure him.

Brother Peck accordingly administered to him and the pain immediately ceased. He slept well during the night and on getting up the next morning played about with his fellows as if nothing had ever been the matter with his arm, not even having it in a sling. The next day he was sent to the doctor to show him his arm, and when he entered his house, the doctor noticed, to his surprise, that the boy took hold of a chair with his lame hand and lifted it forward to sit down upon. Taking the little fellow by the hand, he then asked him if he felt any pain in his arm or hand, and the boy answered frankly that he did not. The doctor bent his fingers and saw that he had free use of them, then examined his hand and wrist and saw that there was no sign of swelling, and declared that it was the power of God which had healed the broken limb, for nothing else could have done it in so short a time. This incident probably influenced Dr. Tate in favor of the Latter-day Saints, as he soon afterwards joined the Church. He was baptized by Elder John E. Page, and ordained an Elder, and for some time was quite a faithful and efficient member, but he subsequently lost the faith. He had abundant evidence, however, while he remained in the Church that the power of God was with the Saints, as he saw it manifested on several occasions so plainly that he could not deny it. But he may have been like some others of whom it has been said that they joined the Church through seeing a miracle performed and apostatized because they could not see one every day.

On one occasion he and Elder Peck were called upon to go a distance of ten miles to see a sister in the Church who was thought to be dying. They traveled with all possible speed, and on arriving at the place found the woman in a very critical condition. The doctor, although used to scenes of sickness, allowed Brother Peck to take the lead in directing what should be done for the relief of the patient, and he proposed to anoint and lay hands upon her. They accordingly did so, and she was healed immediately, and arose and prepared supper for them. While returning home the doctor remarked jocularly, that the experience of that evening presented a new phase in his medical practice. He had never taken that course before to cure patients, nor was he in the habit of going that distance to visit them without charging for it.

While journeying to Missouri with the "Kirtland Camp," Brother Peck's son, Edwin, had his leg accidentally run over by a heavily loaded wagon, on a very hard road. When he was picked up the limb appeared to be flattened as if almost crushed to a pulp, and the flesh was laid open. Brother Peck had seen the power of God manifested in so many instances then, and he had such confidence in the Almighty hearing and answering his prayers, that he never thought of summoning a surgeon, but immediately administered to the boy and then placed him in the wagon. In an hour afterwards he examined his leg and found that it was entirely well, the only sign of the injury left being a slight scar which had the dry and scaly appeaance of an old sore, long since healed up. The place was not even discolored. There were numbers of witnesses to this miracle, many of whom are living to-day.

PHILO DIBBLE'S NARRATIVE.

CHAPTER I.

HIS EARLY LIFE—CONVERSION—CURIOUS SIGNS—JOSEPH REMOVES TO KIRTLAND—WONDERFUL MANIFESTATIONS—A MIRACULOUS CASE OF HEALING—SIDNEY RIGDON IN DARKNESS—JOSEPH PREDICTS THAT THE EVIL ONE WILL HANDLE HIM, AND THE PREDICTION IS FULFILLED.

I AM the second son of Orotor and Bulah Dibble, and was born June 6th, 1806, at Peru, Pittsfield County, Massachusetts. When I was quite young my father removed to the town of Granby, where he died when I was ten years old, leaving my mother with nine children. My elder brother, Philander, and I were taken by one Captain Apollos Phelps, living at Suffield, Connecticut, to raise until we were twenty-one years old, he having no children of his own. Morally speaking, he was a good man, and taught us good principles, and treated us as though we were his own sons.

I remained with him four or five months after I became of age, when I resolved to travel. I then visited Boston, Massachusetts, and its harbor, and saw the ship *Java*, that was fitted out with six hundred soldiers to protect the merchants against the pirates. I also visited several islands and many of the surrounding towns and then returned to Suffield, where I

EARLY LIFE OF ELDER PHILO DIBBLE. 75

became acquainted with Miss Celia Kent, daughter of Benajah Kent, of Suffield, and married her; the Rev. Calvin Phileo performing the ceremony. I was then twenty-three years of age.

My wife having some property in Ohio, we sold our possessions in Connecticut and removed to that part. While crossing Lake Erie from Buffalo to Fairport we encountered a terrible storm, and our destruction seemed imminent, but through an overruling Providence we were saved and landed safely. We passed through Chardon, Ohio, and located three miles west of that city, at a place called King Street, which was within five miles of Kirtland. I there purchased a farm and entered into the business of buying and selling wild lands.

One morning I was standing at my gate when two men drove up in a two-horse wagon, and asked me to get in and go home with them, about quarter of a mile distant. On the way, one asked me if I had heard the news, and informed me that four men had come to Kirtland with a golden Bible and one of them had seen an angel. They laughed and ridiculed the idea, but I did not feel inclined to make light of such a subject. I made no reply, but thought that if angels had administered to the children of men again I was glad of it; I was afraid, however, it was not true. On my return home I told my wife what I had heard.

The next day I was intending to go fifty miles south to the town of Suffield, Ohio, to pay some taxes, but my wife thinking that one or two days would not make much difference about that, proposed that we should hunt up those strange men in Kirtland.

The next morning I took my wife, another man and his wife, and started for Kirtland. When we arrived there, the men we were seeking had gone to the town of Mayfield, but were to return to Kirtland the next day. The following morning I hitched up my carriage and again drove to Kirtland, one of my neighbors accompanying us with his team and family. On arriving there, we were introduced to Oliver Cowdery, Ziba Peterson, Peter Whitmer, Jr., and Parley P. Pratt. I remained with them all day, and became convinced that they were sincere in their professions. I asked Oliver what repentance consisted of, and he replied, "Forsaking sin and yielding obedience to the gospel!"

That evening he preached at Brother Isaac Morley's, and bore his testimony to the administration of an angel at noonday. He then dwelt upon the subjects of repentance and baptism and the bestowal of the Holy Ghost, and promised that all who embraced these principles with honesty of heart should receive a testimony. He also requested all who wished to be baptized to make it manifest by arising. Five persons, among whom were William Cahoon and myself, arose. I then made preparations for baptism by borrowing a suit of clothes. My wife thought I was too hasty, and said if I would wait awhile perhaps she would go along with me. She was a Baptist by persuasion. I paid no heed to her, but went forthwith and was baptized by Parley P. Pratt. This was on the 16th of October, 1830. When I came out of the water, I knew that I had been born of water and of the spirit, for my mind was illuminated with the Holy Ghost.

I spent that evening at Dr. F. G. Williams'. While in bed that night I felt what appeared to be a hand upon my left shoulder and a sensation like fibers of fire immediately enveloped my body. It passed from my right shoulder across my breast to my left shoulder, it then struck me on my collar bone and went to the pit of my stomach, after which it left me. I was enveloped in a heavenly influence, and could not sleep for joy.

The next morning I started home a happy man. All my neighbors were anxious to know the result of my visit to Kirtland, and I was visited by two Campbellite preachers, named respectively Scott and Williams, one of whom remarked, "Mr. Dibble, I understand you have joined the 'Mormons.' What reason have you to believe they have the truth?"

I told them, "The scriptures point to such a work, which should come forth."

He then asked me where I found it. I took the Bible and opened it where it speaks of truth springing out of the earth, and righteousness looking down from above. He read it and handed it to the other preacher. They made no comments.

GIFTS OF THE GOSPEL ENJOYED.

I bore my testimony to them of what I had received, and Mr. Scott said, "I don't doubt, Mr. Dibble, that you have received all you say, because you are honest, but they are impostors."

I then asked Mr. Scott if he believed the Lord would bless the labors of a false prophet, to which they did not stop to reply but left, and told the people it was no use talking to me.

One of my neighbors came to me and said, "We have sent a man down to York State to find out the truth of this work, and he is a man who will not lie. If he returns and says it is false, will you believe him?"

I told him I would believe the truth, and asked him if that man (whose name was Edward Partridge) should come back and say it was false if he would believe him.

He replied, "Yes; for he is a man who would not lie for his right arm!"

I then added, "If he says it is true, will you then believe him?" to which he reluctantly replied that he would.

Shortly after this, however, when Brother Partridge wrote back and said that he had been baptized, and was then preaching the gospel, this man shunned me, and for a long time afterwards gave me no chance to talk with him. But when we met, I asked him what he thought of Brother Partridge, and he replied that he was honest, but had been deceived.

The four missionaries who had visited Kirtland proceeded on westward to the borders of the Lamanites, in Jackson County, Missouri, on the mission to which they had been called by revelation through Joseph the Prophet, leaving the few converts they had made to themselves. Meetings were held occasionally by the members of the Church in Kirtland, all of which I attended. All manner of spirits were there made manifest, and no one to detect them. Many persons were operated upon in a very strange manner, and I was impressed that the spirits which inspired them were from the evil one.

At a meeting held one evening at Brother Whitney's, the heavens were opened and the Spirit of God filled the house and rested upon all the congregation to overflowing, little children not excepted. Prophesying and singing the songs of

Zion were indulged in until morning. Brother Whitney, who had not then yielded obedience to the gospel, was convinced of the truth, and shortly after was baptized.

I will here observe that about the time of which I write, there were many signs and wonders seen in the heavens above and in the earth beneath in the region of Kirtland, both by Saints and strangers. A pillar of light was seen every evening for more than a month hovering over the place where we did our baptizing. One evening also, as Brother William Blakesley and I were returning home from meeting, we observed that it was unusually light, even for moonlight; but, on reflection, we found the moon was not to be seen that night. Although it was cloudy, it was as light as noonday, and we could seemingly see a tree farther that night than we could in the day time.

Soon after this Joseph with his father's family came to Kirtland, and said the Lord had sent him there, and he or the devil would have to leave.

This was the first time I had beheld Joseph. After he arrived the false spirits which had been operating through the members of the Church ceased for awhile.

I held myself in readiness to assist the Smith family with my means or my personal services as they might require, as they were financially poor. They were living on a farm owned by F. G. Williams, in Kirtland, upon which there was a debt of four hundred dollars due, which had to be paid within a stated time or the farm would revert to its former owner.

Joseph Coe, who was required to raise this amount to save the farm, said he could not do so, for his wife held the money and she did not belong to the Church. Being present with Joseph when the subject came up, I said to him, "I can raise the money!" and he replied that if I would, I should be blessed.

I explained to him how I would have to raise the money. I owned twelve hundred acres of land lying twenty miles south of Elyria, which was worth three dollars per acre. In order to raise the money then I would have to sell a portion

A WOMAN WITH A LAME ARM HEALED.

of it for one dollar and twenty-five cents per acre, and I accordingly did so and paid Joseph the four hundred dollars.

When Joseph came to Kirtland his fame spread far and wide. There was a woman living in the town of Hiram, forty miles from Kirtland, who had a crooked arm, which she had not been able to use for a long period. She persuaded her husband, whose name was Johnson, to take her to Kirtland to get her arm healed.

I saw them as they passed my house on their way. She went to Joseph and requested him to heal her. Joseph asked her if she believed the Lord was able to make him an instrument in healing her arm. She said she believed the Lord was able to heal her arm.

Joseph put her off till the next morning, when he met her at Brother Whitney's house. There were eight persons present, one a Methodist preacher, and one a doctor. Joseph took her by the hand, prayed in silence a moment, pronounced her arm whole, in the name of Jesus Christ, and turned and left the room.

The preacher asked her if her arm was whole, and she straightened it out and replied: "It is as good as the other." The question was then asked if it would remain whole. Joseph hearing this, answered and said: "It is as good as the other, and as liable to accident as the other."

The doctor who witnessed this miracle came to my house the next morning and related the circumstance to me. He attempted to account for it by his false philosophy, saying that Joseph took her by the hand, and seemed to be in prayer, and pronounced her arm whole in the name of Jesus Christ, which excited her and started perspiration, and that relaxed the cords of her arm.

I subsequently rented my farm and devoted all my time to the interest of the Church, holding myself in readiness to take Joseph wherever he wished to go.

On invitation of Father Johnson, of Hiram, Joseph removed his family to his home, to translate the New Testament. This was in the year 1831.

At this time Sidney Rigdon was left to preside at Kirtland and frequently preached to us. Upon one occasion he said the keys of the kingdom were taken from us. On hearing this, many of his hearers wept, and when some one undertook to dismiss the meeting by prayer he said praying would do them no good, and the meeting broke up in confusion.

Brother Hyrum came to my house the next morning and told me all about it, and said it was false, and that the keys of the kingdom were still with us. He wanted my carriage and horses to go to the town of Hiram and bring Joseph. The word went abroad among the people immediately that Sidney was going to expose "Mormonism."

Joseph came up to Kirtland a few days afterwards and held a meeting in a large barn. Nearly all the inhabitants of Kirtland turned out to hear him. The barn was filled with people, and others, unable to get inside, stood around the door as far as they could hear.

Joseph arose in our midst and spoke in mighty power, saying: "I can contend with wicked men and devils—yes with angels. No power can pluck those keys from me, except the power that gave them to me; that was Peter, James and John. But for what Sidney has done, the devil shall handle him as one man handles another."

Thomas B. Marsh's wife went from the meeting and told Sidney what Joseph had said, and he replied: "Is it possible that I have been so deceived? But if Joseph says so, it is so."

About three weeks after this, Sidney was lying on his bed alone. An unseen power lifted him from his bed, thew him across the room, and tossed him from one side of the room to the other. The noise being heard in the adjoining room, his family went in to see what was the matter, and found him going from one side of the room to the other, from the effects of which Sidney was laid up for five or six weeks. Thus was Joseph's prediction in regard to him verified.

When Joseph was ready to go back to Hyrum, I took him in my carriage. Soon afterwards I had occasion to visit Hyrum again. On my way there I was persuaded to stop at the Hulet settlement and attend a meeting. When I arrived at Father Johnson's the next morning, Joseph and Sidney had just finished washing up from being tared and feathered the night before. Joseph said to Sidney: "We can now go on our mission to Jackson County" (alluding to a commandment given them while they were translating, but which they concluded not to attend to until they had finished that work). I felt to regret very much that I had not been with them the evening before, but it was perhaps providential that I was not. On a subsequent visit to Hiram, I arrived at Father Johnson's just as Joseph and Sidney were coming out of the vision alluded to in the Book of Doctrine and Covenants, in which mention is made of the three glories. Joseph wore black clothes, but at this time seemed to be dressed in an element of glorious white, and his face shone as if it were transparent, but I did not see the same glory attending Sidney. Joseph appeared as strong as a lion, but Sidney seemed as weak as water, and Joseph, noticing his condition smiled and said, "Brother Sidney is not as used to it as I am."

CHAPTER II.

REMOVAL TO MISSOURI—THE SAINTS' GUNS PURCHASED FOR MOBOCRATS BY A SECTARIAN PREACHER—ATTACK OF THE MOB ON THE WHITMER SETTLEMENT—THE WRITER SHOT—SUBSEQUENT EXPOSURE AND SUFFERING—CRITICAL CONDITION—HEALED MIRACULOUSLY—HOW ZION'S CAMP WAS PRESERVED ON FISHING RIVER—A VISION.

IN 1832 I sold my possessions in Ohio, and, we being called upon by Joseph to advance monies to purchase the land in Jackson County, I paid fifty dollars for that purpose and also gave Brother Parley P. Pratt fifty dollars to assist him as a pioneer. I was then called on for money to be placed in the hands of Brothers Whitney and Gilbert, who were going to New York to purchase goods to take up to Jackson County, and gave them three hundred dollars.

I joined in with a company led by Brother Thomas B. Marsh, and arrived in Independence, Jackson County, on the

10th of November. I remained in Independence until spring and then removed to the Whitmer settlement, farther west, where I built a house, fenced twenty acres of land and put in a garden.

In the fall of 1833, a sectarian preacher by the name of M'Coy came to the Whitmer settlement where I was living to buy up all the guns he could, representing that he wanted them for the Indians. We suspected no trouble, and quite a number of us sold our guns to him. The sequel of his action was, however, soon apparent to us, for rumors soon reached us of mobs assembling and threats being made to drive us from the County.

When the mob first began to gather and threaten us, I was selected to go to another County and buy powder and lead. The brethren gave me the privilege of choosing a man to go with me. I took with me a man by the name of John Poorman. We thought we were good for four of the mob. We went to the town of Liberty, Clay County, and purchased the ammunition, and returned safely.

Soon after I returned a mob of about one hundred and fifty came upon us in the dead hour of night, tore down a number of our houses and whipped and abused several of our brethren. I was aroused from my sleep by the noise caused by the falling houses, and had barely time to escape to the woods with my wife and two children when they reached my house and proceeded to break in the door and tear the roof off. I was some distance away from where the whipping occurred, but I heard the blows of heavy ox goads upon the backs of my brethren distinctly. The mob also swore they would tear down our grist mill, which was situated at the Colesville branch, about three miles from the settlement, and lest they should really do so, and as it was the only means we had of getting our grain ground, we were counseled to gather there and defend it. We accordingly proceeded there the next morning. The following night two men came into our camp, pretending they wanted to hire some men to work for them. Brother Parley ordered them to be taken prisoners, when one of them struck him a glancing blow on the head with his gun, inflicting a severe wound. We then disarmed them and kept them as prisoners until morning when we gave them back their arms and let them go.

The next day we heard firing down in the Whitmer settlement, and seventeen of our brethren volunteered to go down and see what it meant. Brother George Beebe was one of these volunteers and also one of the men who was whipped the night previous.* When these seventeen men arrived at the Whitmer settlement, the mob came against them and took some prisoners. Brother David Whitmer brought us the news of this and said: "Every man go, and every man take a man!"

We all responded and met the mob in battle, in which I was wounded with an ounce ball and two buck shot, all entering my body just at the right side of my navel. The mob were finally routed, and the brethren chased them a mile away. Several others of the brethren were also shot, and one, named Barber, was mortally wounded. After the battle was over, some of the brethren went to administer to him, but he objected to their praying that he might live, and asked them if they could not see the angels present. He said the room was full of them, and his greatest anxiety was for his friends to see what he saw, until he breathed his last, which occurred at three o'clock in the morning.

A young lawyer named Bazill, who came into Independence and wanted to make himself conspicuous, joined the mob, and swore he would wade in blood up to his chin.

He was shot with two balls through his head, and never spoke. There was another man, whose name I fail to remember, that lived on the Big Blue, who made a similar boast. He was also taken at his word. His chin was shot off, or so badly fractured by a ball that he was forced to have it amputated, but lived and recovered, though he was a horrible sight afterwards.

After the battle I took my gun and powder horn and started for home. When I got about half way I became faint and thirsty. I wanted to stop at Brother Whitmer's to lay down. The house, however, was full of women and children, and.

---

*——Brother Beebe carried the marks of this whipping to his grave, as the brethren who laid him out at the time of his death, in December, 1881, at Provo, Utah County, can testify.

they were so frightened that they objected to my entering, as the mob had threatened that wherever they found a wounded man they would kill men, women and children.

I continued on and arrived home, or rather at a house in the field that the mob had not torn down, which was near my own home. There I found my wife and two children and a number of other women who had assembled. I told them I was shot and wanted to lay down.

They got me on the bed, but on thinking of what the mob had said, became frightened, and assisted me up stairs. I told them, however, that I could not stay there, my pain was so great. They then got me down stairs again, and my wife went out to see if she could find any of the brethren. In searching for them she got lost in the woods and was gone two hours, but learned that all the brethren had gone to the Colesville branch, three miles distant, taking all the wounded with them save myself.

The next morning I was taken farther off from the road, that I might be concealed from the mob. I bled inwardly until my body was filled with blood, and remained in this condition until the next day at five p. m. I was then examined by a surgeon who was in the Black Hawk war, and who said that he had seen a great many men wounded, but never saw one wounded as I was that ever lived. He pronounced me a dead man.

David Whitmer, however, sent me word that I should live and not die, but I could see no possible chance to recover. After the surgeon had left me, Brother Newell Knight came to see me, and sat down on the side of my bed. He laid his right hand on my head, but never spoke. I felt the Spirit resting upon me at the crown of my head before his hand touched me, and I knew immediately that I was going to be healed. It seemed to form like a ring under the skin, and followed down my body. When the ring came to the wound, another ring formed around the first bullet hole, also the second and third. Then a ring formed on each shoulder and on each hip, and followed down to the ends of my fingers and toes and left me. I immediately arose and discharged three quarts of blood or more, with some pieces of my clothes that had been driven into my body by the bullets. I then dressed myself and went out doors and saw the falling of the stars, which so encouraged the Saints and frightened their enemies. It was one of the grandest sights I ever beheld. From that time not a drop of blood came from me and I never afterwards felt the slightest pain or inconvenience from my wounds, except that I was somewhat weak from the loss of blood.

The next day I walked around the field, and the day following I mounted a horse and rode eight miles, and went three miles on foot.

The night of the battle many of the women and children ran into the woods. One sister, not being able to take all of her children with her, left her little boy four years old in a corn shock, where he remained until morning. Some went out on the burnt prairie. The mob gathered and swore they would go and massacre them. When they got ready to go, the heavens were lit up with the falling of stars. This brought to us a perfect redemption at that time.

The night of the battle, the mob took all my household furniture, and after my recovery I crossed the river to Clay County, leaving behind me a drove of hogs, three cows and all of my crop, which I never recovered.

In Clay County I enjoyed some rest from persecution, and had two children born to me, Emma and Philo, Jun. I was there when Zion's camp came up. I met them on Fishing river. There the power of the Lord was manifested by His sending a thunder storm, which raised Fishing river ten feet higher than it was ever known to rise before. I saw the cloud coming up in the west when I was ten miles from Fishing river in the middle of the afternoon. As it moved on eastwardly it increased in size and in blackness, and when it got over the camp it stopped, and in the night the rain and hail poured down in torrents, and the lightning flashed from the cloud continuously for three hours.

Just before night, two men came into camp and asked where Mr. Smith was. Joseph said, "I am the man." They then advised him to disband his camp, "for," said they, "the mob are gathering, and there won't be one of you left to-morrow morning!"

Joseph smiled, and said: "I guess not." Seeing that Joseph did not believe what they came to tell him, they went off vexed.

We learned afterwards that the hail was so heavy on the mob, that they were forced to seek shelter, and the leader of them swore he would never go against the "Mormons" again.

Zion's camp was disbanded on Fishing river. The leading men of Liberty being desirous for peace, called a meeting and invited our leading men to meet with them, which they did. They told our committee that if they could have peace, we should have a County to ourselves, and if we had not money enough to buy out the old settlers of Caldwell County they would lend us money to buy them out.

This settled our difficulties at that time.

In the meantime a conference was held in Liberty, Clay County, at which I was ordained a Teacher under the hands of David Whitmer.

We then commenced settling Caldwell County, to which I removed, built a house, entered seven hundred and twenty acres of land and bought a lot in town. I also entered land for many of the brethren, and for this purpose had to go the distance of eighty miles, where the land office was located.

On my return home, when I got to Liberty, midway between Lexington and Far West, I concluded I would travel from there home by night, as it was very warm during the day. The road led through a strip of timber for four miles, and after that across a prairie for twenty miles.

When I had traveled about two-thirds of the way across the prairie, riding on horseback, I heard the cooing of the prairie hens. I looked northward and saw, apparently with my natural vision, a beautiful city, the streets of which ran north and south. I also knew there were streets running east and west, but could not trace them with my eye for the buildings. The walks on each side of the streets were as white as marble, and the trees on the outer side of the marble walks had the appearance of locust trees in autumn. This city was in view for about one hour-and-a-half, as near as I could judge, as I traveled along. When I began to descend towards the Crooked river the timber through which I passed hid the city from my view. Every block in this mighty city had sixteen spires, four on each corner, each block being built in the form of a hollow square, within which I seemed to know that the gardens of the inhabitants were situated. The corner buildings on which the spires rested were larger and higher than the others, and the several blocks were uniformly alike. The beauty and grandeur of the scene I cannot describe. While viewing the city the buildings appeared to be transparent. I could not discern the inmates, but I appeared to understand that they could discern whatever passed outside.

Whether this was a city that has been or is to be I cannot tell. It extended as far north as Adam-ondi-Ahman, a distance of about twenty-eight miles. Whatever is revealed to us by the Holy Ghost will never be forgotten.

CHAPTER III.

MILITIA ORGANIZED AT FAR WEST—LIBERTY POLE STRUCK BY LIGHTNING — GENERAL ATCHISON DEFENDS THE PROPHET IN A LAWSUIT—ATCHISON REMOVED FROM OFFICE FOR BEING FRIENDLY TO THE SAINTS—FAR WEST BESIEGED—BETRAYED FOR A PRICE—ESCAPE TO QUINCY.

PART of Zion's camp went back to Kirtland, and also Brother Joseph, but in consequence of the mobs and apostates the Church organization in Kirtland was broken up. Some of the apostates left Kirtland and came up to Far West. They called meetings and told the people that Joseph was a fallen prophet, and they were determined to put David Whitmer in his place. Some of the brethren, including the president of the branch I lived in, fell in with the views of the apostates. I being a Teacher in the branch, took up a labor with them, first going to our president and taking with me a Deacon. Our president said if he had got to become an enemy to David to be a friend to Joseph, he could not be a friend to Joseph. He then called the branch together in order to put me out of office as a Teacher, but the branch sustained me. He afterwards cited me to appear for trial before Bishop Partridge, who gave me two weeks to make satisfaction, and I appealed my case to the High Council, who decided there was no cause of action.

Joseph and family soon arrived at Far West. Soon after a regiment was organized by W. W. Phelps, Geo. M. Hinkle, Lyman Wight and Reed Peck, they having received their commissions from the governor. An election of officers was called and G. W. Robinson was elected colonel, I lieutenant colonel and Seymour Brunson major.

While celebrating the 4th of July at Far West, there came up a thunder shower, and the lightning struck our liberty pole and shivered it to pieces. Joseph walked around on the splinters and said: "As that pole was splintered, so shall the nations of the earth be!"

When the trouble with the mob commenced, Colonel Robinson took about one-half of the force to Adam-ondi-Ahman to defend that place. Joseph, Hyrum and Sidney also went with them, leaving me in command at Far West. The detachment returned in about four days.

A few days afterwards Joseph Smith and I took a walk out upon the prairie, and in the course of our conversation I suggested to him to send for General Atchison to defend him in the suit then brought against him, as he was in command of the third division of the militia of the State of Missouri, and was a lawyer and a friend to law. Joseph made no reply, but turned back immediately to Far West, and a man was selected, with the best horse to be found, to go to Liberty for General Atchison.

The next day General Atchison came to Far West with a hundred men and camped a little north of the town.

On consulting with Joseph Smith, Atchison told him that he did not want any one to go with them to his trial, which was to take place midway between Far West and Adam-ondi-Ahman. Joseph at first hesitated about agreeing to this, but Atchison reassured him by saying: "My life for yours!"

When they arrived at the place of trial quite a number of the mob had gathered, and on seeing Joseph commenced to curse and swear. Atchison, however, checked them by saying: "Hold on boys, if you fire the first gun there will not be one of you left!"

Joseph was cleared and came away unmolested. Soon afterwards the governor, thinking Atchison was too friendly towards the Saints, took his command from him and placed General Clark in command of the militia.

Shortly before Far West was besieged, I was taken sick, and Colonel Hinkle came into military command under his old commission. I gave up my horse, saddle and bridle, and also my rifle and sword for Brother Lysander Gee to use in defense of our city.

When General Clark's army came up against Far West, Colonel Hinkle betrayed the First Presidency of the Church into their hands for seven hundred and fifty dollars. Then Joseph and Hyrum, Sidney, and Lyman Wight were taken by the mob, who held a court-martial over them and sentenced them to be shot the next morning at eight o'clock on the public square. Lyman Wight told them to "shoot and be damned." Generals Atchison and Doniphan immediately rebelled against the decision, and Doniphan said, if men were to be murdered in cold blood, he would withdraw his troops, which he did. General Atchison then went to Liberty and gave a public dinner, and delivered a speech, in which he said, "If the governor does not restore my commission to me, I will kill him, so help me God!" On hearing this the audience became so enthusiastic that they took him upon their shoulders and carried him around the public square.

After the surrender of Far West, the mob sent officers to get me, but finding that I was sick they went back and so reported. They came the second time and went back and reported the same. The third time they came they swore they would have me if they had to take me on a bed. I lived one-and-a-half miles west of the town, and told my folks if they could dress me and help me on my horse I would undertake to leave for Quincy. A young man named Joel Miles was to go with me to help me off and on my horse. Leaving Far West on my left, I arrived at Quincy unmolested.

I will here digress from my narrative, and state that while I was at Far West the battle of Crooked river occurred, in which David W. Patten was killed, also the massacre at Haun's Mill. Brother Joseph had sent word by Haun, who owned the mill, to inform the brethren who were living there to leave and come to Far West, but Mr. Haun did not deliver the message. I should also have mentioned that while at Far West an election was held to elect an assessor. Isaac Higbee, myself and a Missourian were the candidates. The brethren held a caucus meeting and advised one of us to withdraw our name lest the Missourian might gain the election, and proposed that Higbee and I cast lots for it. Two tickets were put into a hat for us to draw from. There was a large crowd gathered around and Joseph Smith among them. He said, "I am going to prophesy that Philo will get it." Sure enough I drew it.

On my arrival in Quincy, knowing that our people would soon be flocking there in great numbers to cross the river, I rented the ferry at nine dollars per day for thirty days. I ran the boat about ten days and ferried the Saints across on their own terms, and still made money at it. Some of the brethren, however, on arriving, assumed the right to dictate me, and wanted that I should give up the ferry into their hands. The man who owned it said if I would give it up he would release me from paying that day's rent, which I agreed to do, supposing it would go into the hands of the brethren. But when I gave up the papers to him, he informed the brethren that they must pay him full fare or else make boats and ferry themselves at half price. This caused a great deal of extra and unnecessary expense to our people.

Before I left Far West, I made arrangements with a man to bring my family through to Quincy, for which I paid him sixty dollars in gold on their arrival.

In the spring of 1839, Sidney Rigdon came to me and said he knew of a man who owned a farm three miles east of Quincy and wanted to rent it to some good man whom he could recommend, and that I could have the chance. I gladly accepted the offer and rented the farm of two hundred acres.

CHAPTER IV.

SUCCESSFUL FARMING—SICKNESS—PROVIDENTIAL RECOVERY—INSPIRED TO PREACH—REMOVAL TO NAUVOO—DEATH OF MY WIFE—SECOND MARRIAGE—PREMONITION OF DEATH—WARNING FROM THE PROPHET—A DREAM AND ITS FULFILLMENT—A PROPHECY AND ITS FULFILLMENT—EVIL SPIRITS CAST OUT OF A MAN—JOSEPH SMITH'S TRUST IN THE LORD.

I TOOK four other brethren—Simeon Crandall and three of his sons, to help me carry on the farm, and we raised a heavy crop, which took us all the fall and winter to market.

While living upon this farm, I was taken sick. Dr. Williams attended me, and after awhile said he could do no more for me. I then called for the Elders to administer to me and Brother A. J. Stewart, his brother, Levi, and Brother Killian were called in, but before they arrived Mr. Robbins, of whom I rented the farm, called to see me. He declared that I might possibly live till three o'clock, but could not live till morning.

When the Elders administered to me, Brother Killian being mouth, I was in bed. He poured the oil on my forehead and I jumped right out of bed and put on my clothes. On hearing that Robbins was going to Quincy in the morning, I walked up to his house, three-quarters of a mile, and went with him in his carriage to Quincy, remained all day and returned with him at night.

Some of my gentile neighbors, wishing to learn about "Mormonism," sent to Quincy for Brother John P. Greene to come out and preach to them. When he came, he called at my house and wanted to know of me what subject he had better treat upon. I told him were I in his place I should speak on the resurrection of the dead, which he did. There was a large congregation of members of various denominations present. They were so well pleased with Brother Greene's remarks, that they would not let him off until he left another appointment to preach. Before the appointed time arrived, however, Brother Greene was taken sick and could not come. A large congregation had gathered at the place appointed, and only three Elders present—A. J. Stewart, his brother Levi, and myself.

Seeing the situation of things, we consulted together as to what should be done, when Brother A. J. Stewart said he would undertake to fill Brother Greene's appointment, but that if he got baulked we must help him out. I remarked I could not preach, if I did it would only be like a sectarian telling his experience, but said, "1 will do the singing," which I did.

Brother Stewart arose, opened the Bible and tried to read, but had to spell his words, and broke down and said that some of the brethren would take up the subject and go on with it. He then called on me. I arose to speak. The Holy Ghost came down and enveloped me, and I spoke for over two hours. When I found the Spirit leaving me I thought it time to close, and told my hearers it was the first time I had spoken to a public congregation.

A Brother Mills who was present, felt so well that he went home with me and declared that I had delivered the greatest discourse he had ever heard. Said I: "Brother Mills, I don't know what I have said. It was not me; it was the Lord!"

In the spring of 1840, I removed to Nauvoo, then called Commerce, which had been appointed by Joseph for the gathering place. During the next year my wife died, and left me with five children, two daughters and three sons. I concluded to get my children homes and then travel and preach the gospel; but when I had obtained homes for them I found I had not only lost my wife, but also my children, and they had not only lost their mother, but also their father and each other's society.

On the 11th of February, 1841, I married a second wife—a Widow Smith of Philadelphia, who was living in the family of the Prophet. He performed the ceremony at his house, and Sister Emma Smith insisted upon getting up a wedding supper for us. It was a splendid affair, and quite a large party of our friends were assembled.

I then rented a house of Hyrum Kimball on the river bank for ten dollars per month, and kept a warehouse, and also boarders and a bakery. While there in business, I saw in vision my grave before me for two weeks; it mattered not whether my eyes were open or shut it was there, and I saw no way of escape. One day Brother Joseph came and took dinner with us, and as we arose from the table I walked out upon the porch and sat down on a bench. Joseph and my wife followed me, and he came before me and said: "Philo, you must get away from here or you will die, as sure as God ever spoke by my mouth!" He then turned to my wife and said: "And you will hardly escape by the skin of your teeth!"

I immediately stepped into Joseph's carriage and rode with him to the south part of town and rented another place, after which I settled up my business as fast as I could, and made arrangements to remove. Many hearing of Joseph's prediction about me, said if they had been in my place they would have remained where I was and tested the truth of it, but I assured them if they had been in my place they would have done just as I did.

After I had settled my business and removed my family, we were one day at Joseph's house, when he said to my wife: "You didn't believe what I told Philo the other day! Now, I will tell you what the Lord told me; He told me to go and tell Philo to come away from there, and if he obeyed he should live; if not he should die; and I didn't want to see you a widow so soon again. If Philo had remained there fourteen days longer, he would have been a corpse."

One night Joseph came to my house about twelve o'clock, and called me up. I immediately went out to see what was wanted. We went across the street to James Allred's and called him up, and we three went back to Joseph's house. On the way he told us that a flat boat with about thirty men had landed just below his house, and that he had overheard some of their conversation. They had made arrangements to kidnap him that night and sink him in the river. Brother Allred and I went down to the river; but they must have seen Joseph's movements as we found nothing of them, although we got up some more of the brethren and searched up and down the river.

When Joseph and Emma were preparing to go up the river to Dixon, to make a visit with some of her connections, I was at their house. The night before they started, I had a dream, in which I saw Joseph taken prisoner and guarded by two men, who after awhile left Joseph in Nauvoo and went off cursing and swearing. The next morning I related my dream to Joseph; he listened to me but made no reply.

While visiting at Dixon he was taken prisoner by a sheriff of Missouri and an officer of Illinois, but instead of getting him over into Missouri as they had planned to, he was brought to Nauvoo. There they left Joseph and went off cursing and swearing, just as I had heard them in my dream.

When, on the advice of the Prophet, I quit my situation on the river, my wife felt so bad at the loss of my business prospects that she said we might as well die by the sword as by famine. I asked her if she thought it would be worse for us temporally to obey the word of the Lord. I prophesied that before the year would pass away it would be better for us than if we had remained there.

Wm. Pratt had three city lots upon which he was owing a debt of one hundred dollars, and said if I would raise the money I might have my choice of the three. I raised the money all but three dollars, but was at a loss to know how to get the balance. It was a hard time to borrow money. On my way to Brother Pratt's, I picked up three dollars in the street, Brother Stephen Goddard being with me at the time.

I then took the three dollar bill which I found to Bishop Whitney's and requested him to take the number of it, and if an owner came for it to say that I would refund it to him, but that I wanted the use of it a few days. I soon sold the lot for four hundred dollars, and then asked my wife if my prophecy was not fulfilled.

One of my neighbors, a Brother James Moses, who lived across the street from me, was taken sick, and for six weeks was not able to speak above his breath. I went occasionally to see him, and one day while there Brother Bills and I were asked by Sister Moses to administer to him, which we did. She then asked us what we thought of him, and I replied that I had no testimony that he would live or that he would die; but she might as well pour water upon fire to make it burn as to give him medicine. This offended her, as she had a doctor by the name of Green attending him, and we left.

Soon after this Brother Kimball (one of the Apostles) was called on to administer to him, when Sister Moses asked him what he thought of her husband's condition. He replied in the very words that I had used, but advised them to hold on to him. Brother Bills and I happening to call in again to see him, we were asked if we would anoint him. I consented and stepped up to the bed to put some oil on his forehead, but felt impressed to stop and say that he was possessed of evil spirits, and that they would kill him if they were not cast out before morning. He then commenced raving, and might have been heard across the street.

The Twelve Apostles were sent for and three of them came, Brother W. Richards being one of them, who was mouth in prayer, as we all knelt in the room. After prayer, Brother Richards went to the bed, and, in the name of Jesus Christ, commanded the evil spirits to leave him and leave the house, which they did instantly, and Brother Moses became rational. He afterwards told us all about his feelings while the evil spirits had afflicted him, and that he was as sore as a boil all over from the effects of what he had passed through.

When Joseph first came to Nauvoo, then called Commerce, a Mr. White, living there, proffered to sell him his farm for twenty-five hundred dollars, five hundred dollars of the amount to be paid down, and the balance one year from that time. Joseph and the brethren were talking about this offer when some of them said: "We can't buy it, for we lack the money." Joseph took out his purse, and, emptying out its contents, offered a half dollar to one of the brethren, which he declined accepting, but Joseph urged him to take it, and then gave each of the other brethren a similar amount, which left him without any. Addressing the brethren, he then said: "Now you all have money, and I have none; but the time will come when I will have money and you will have none!" He then said to Bishop Knight: "You go back and buy the farm!"

Brother Knight went to White, but learned from him that he had raised the price one hundred dollars, and returned to Joseph without closing the bargain. Joseph again sent him with positive orders to purchase, but Brother Knight, finding that White had raised the price still another hundred dollars, again returned without purchasing. For the third time then Joseph commanded him to go and buy the farm, and charged him not to come back till he had done so.

When Bishop Knight got back to White, he had raised another hundred on the place, making the whole amount twenty-eight hundred dollars. However, the bargain was closed and the obligations drawn up, but how the money was going to be raised neither Brother Knight nor the other Brethren could see. The next morning Joseph and several of the brethren went down to Mr. White's to sign the agreement and make the first payment on the land. A table was brought out with the papers upon it, and Joseph signed them, moved back from the table and sat with his head down, as if in thought for a moment. Just then a man drove up in a carriage and asked if Mr. Smith was there. Joseph hearing it, got up and went to the door. The man said, "Good morning, Mr. Smith; I am on a speculation to-day. I want to buy some land, and thought I would come and see you." Joseph then pointed around where his land lay, but the man said: "I can't go with you to-day to see the land. Do you want any money this morning?"

Joseph replied that he would like some, and when the stranger asked "How much?" he told him "Five hundred dollars."

The man walked into the house with Joseph, emptied a small sack of gold on the table, and counted out that amount. He then handed to Joseph another hundred dollars, saying: "Mr. Smith, I make you a present of this!"

After this transpired, Joseph laughed at the brethren and said: "You trusted in money; but I trusted in God. Now I have money and you have none."

www.ingramcontent.com/pod-product-compliance
Lightning Source LLC
Chambersburg PA
CBHW032238080426
42735CB00008B/908